Open Doors!

Open Doors!
A Proven Guide for Reaching Your Highest Potential and Achieving Your Dreams

Yitzchak Pierson

Published by Game Changer Publishing

Paperback ISBN: 978-1-962656-20-7
Hardcover ISBN: 978-1-962656-21-4
Digital: ISBN: 978-1-962656-22-1

www.GameChangerPublishing.com

DEDICATION

I would like to thank my mom, Patricia, my sisters Rachel, Moriah, Abigail, and Ana, my brother-in-law Seth, brother-in-law Robert, and my nieces and nephews. They are my WHY. They are a major part of why I work hard every day. I want to be a good example and to create a future where we can all thrive and create beautiful memories together.

I would also like to thank my mentor, Colum, and first coach, Dr. Caitlin Walker, and my current Coach, Jeff Rubenstein.

Thank you to Brian Mayoral and his company SellUp and Troy Wahl for believing in my highest potential and not just my current circumstances.

I'd also like to thank my best friend Mitchell, who has always been an inspiration to me in his pursuit of perfecting his craft as a musician. Throughout all of the changes in my life, he's always been there to listen to me and see me at my best and at my worst.

I would also like to thank my friend Michele Schalin for writing her book *Mindful Metamorphosis*. She helped inspire me to write this book.

I would also like to thank my dad because I would not be who I am without the adversity I've overcome. There are so many other people who have been a major part of my success, so thank you all. You know who you are. I am extremely grateful for the opportunities and the open doors.

Read This First

Just to say thanks for buying and reading my book, I would like to give you a free welcome call with me, no strings attached!

Simply Scan the QR Code Here:

Open Doors!

A Proven Guide for Reaching Your Highest

Potential and Achieving Your Dreams

Yitzchak Pierson

www.GameChangerPublishing.com

Foreword

Yitzchak Pierson is many things - REALTOR®, educator, coach - and in his debut as an author, he weaves his pathway to all of these identities with the unique and compelling story of where he started his journey. *Open Doors!* combines an index of self-help approaches, goal-setting practices, and frameworks with the narrative of how Yitzchak went from fighting to receive his social security card to achieving multiple professional accolades and distinctions. His clear and robust desire to better himself and to pay it forward is evident in every word of his book and in his daily practice for those who have grown to know him.

When I first met and coached Yitzchak, he was early in his journey. He was a newly minted realtor who had navigated personal and professional hardships to make major life and work changes. In our time working together, he further defined his professional values and goals and established a personal and professional brand through in-person networking and digital marketing. We also collaborated on him securing and preparing for his first speaking engagement. In the few short years since then, he has become a rising star in his field and a coach in his own right.

In reading *Open Doors!,* you'll gain not just curated resources to help you on your personal journey to reach your potential and achieve your dreams but will also receive anecdotes and insights from someone who has been consistently committed to doing the same. It can be easy to relish where you have traveled to without looking back to where you started. Yitzchak's vulnerability in sharing the long journey of his young life so far will further enrich your understanding of the transformative power of consistency and dedication.

Open Doors! will likely also challenge your self-limiting beliefs and expose the ways that the version of your story you have told yourself is no longer serving or empowering you. I hope that by learning more about Yitzchak's journey, the tools he's leveraged along the way, and the challenges he overcame, you can reconcile where you've been with where you want to be next.

Lastly, I commend Yitzchak on this venture. I will always remember the day he and I discussed the weight of perceptions. I told him that his story had power and that while his ambitions were admirable, providing the context for his achievements would help others not just understand him better, but also understand themselves and their own capacity better. I believe that you will do both as you begin to *Open Doors!* in your learning, work, and life.

– Dr. Caitlin Walker, PT, DPT, MBA & Owner, Business Operations
& Development Consultant at DRC Development

Endorsement

Great read from cover to cover! A captivating story about dealing with life's challenges of adversity, scarcity, and trauma and how Yitzchak has been able to use his life experiences and setbacks to become a successful entrepreneur and someone who has figured out what's most important in life. This book provides actual real-life scenarios that many people face every day and some that most people will never experience.

– Jeff Rubenstein, REALTOR® & SUCCESS Coach

Table of Contents

THE RABBIT HOLE JOURNEY

I want to start the book by asking you to be open-minded. Hopefully, this book will send you down a rabbit hole to learn more and provide you with the knowledge to take actionable steps, opening doors to turn your wildest dreams into reality. I realize how little I know in this world, but I want to impart some of the things I have learned in hopes that it will benefit you or someone you know.

Thank you in advance for reading this book and for giving me grace and understanding because I will be very vulnerable in this book. However, I feel that vulnerability is needed to help people to the fullest of my abilities. The more you know about someone, where they came from, and what they went through to accomplish their current level of success, the more believable and achievable it is for you to accomplish your goals and the level of success you desire.

One of my favorite sayings from Damon West is, "You are uniquely positioned to best serve the person you once were." I hope to help those who feel stuck or who are searching for more out of life! Keep searching and taking action every day!

"You don't know what you don't know."

The phrase "you don't know what you don't know" is a way to describe a state of unawareness about something. It encapsulates a

1

situation where an individual lacks knowledge in a particular area and is unaware of their lack of knowledge. Here's a detailed breakdown of what this phrase means:

1. Unawareness of the Subject Matter:

The individual does not have knowledge or awareness of a particular subject, concept, or skill. They are oblivious to the fact that this knowledge even exists or that it is relevant.

2. Lack of Recognition of the Deficit:

Beyond not having the knowledge, the individual does not recognize that they are missing this knowledge. This is different from knowing that you lack understanding in a particular area. In this state, you aren't even aware that there is something to know.

3. Relation to the Unconscious Incompetence Stage:

This phrase is often associated with the first stage of the Four Stages of Competence, known as Unconscious Incompetence. In this stage, a person is unaware of a skill and their deficiency in that skill. They need help understanding the skill, how to do it, or even that it is something they should learn.

4. Potential Risks and Challenges:

Being in a state where "you don't know what you don't know" can lead to oversights, misunderstandings, and mistakes, especially in complex or specialized fields. Without awareness of a knowledge gap, a person might not seek out the necessary education or resources to fill that gap.

5. Opportunities for Growth and Discovery:

While this state can present challenges, it also represents an opportunity for growth, learning, and discovery. Once a person becomes aware of what they don't know (moving into the Conscious Incompetence stage), they can begin the process of learning and personal or professional development.

Conclusion:

The phrase "you don't know what you don't know" reminds us of the limits of our knowledge and the potential blind spots in our understanding. It encourages humility, curiosity, and a willingness to recognize that there may be important areas of knowledge or skill that we have yet to explore or even identify. This concept can be particularly relevant in coaching, education, and self-improvement contexts, where uncovering unknown areas of ignorance can lead to significant growth and development.

The Four Stages of Competence:

These stages describe the psychological states involved in progressing from incompetence to competence in a particular skill. Here's a formal and detailed explanation of each stage:

1. Unconscious Incompetence:

This is the stage where an individual is unaware of the skill and their lack of proficiency. They need help understanding or knowing how to execute the skill, and they do not necessarily recognize the deficit. A person in this stage may need to recognize their own incompetence before moving on to the next stage.

2. Conscious Incompetence:

At this stage, the individual becomes aware of the existence and relevance of the skill and recognizes a deficiency in their ability. Although they understand or know how to execute the skill, they are consciously aware of their inability to do so proficiently. This awareness may lead to frustration, but it is an essential step toward acquiring the skill. Practice, commitment, and the willingness to learn are required to move to the next stage.

3. Conscious Competence:

The individual understands the skill and knows how to perform it. However, performing the skill requires concentration, effort, and conscious thinking. It is not yet an automated activity. Continued practice and conscious effort to refine the skill are essential in this stage. Feedback and self-correction are often necessary to become more proficient.

4. Unconscious Competence:

In this final stage, the individual has practiced the skill to the point where it can be performed without conscious thought. It becomes an automatic response and can be executed with ease and efficiency. This level of competence often leads to the skill being performed intuitively and fluidly, and the individual may even be able to teach it to others.

The Four Stages of Competence model provides a useful framework for understanding the progression of learning and skill acquisition. It can be applied to various domains, including personal development, professional growth, and educational contexts. By recognizing the stage they are in, individuals can take targeted actions to progress through these stages and achieve mastery in a particular skill or area of knowledge.

CHAPTER 1

THE CULT LIFE

The best way to start this story is by providing a little background on my dad so that you know more about how he became a "pastor/apostle/ prophet," or, in the simplest terms, a Cult Leader. As far as I know, he had a pretty normal childhood. He grew up in San Antonio, Texas, and his parents divorced when he was three years old – Karen and Bill. Karen remarried Barry shortly after, and Barry adopted my father. A few years down the road, my aunt Paula was born. Now, my dad did say that Barry was a drinker and somewhat abusive, so my grandma Karen would often send him to his room to avoid run-ins with Barry. But my dad said there were good times as well.

My dad often spent time in Kansas as he got older with his grandmother and cousins on Karen's side of the family. He said she was much stricter but also loving, an old-school tough woman. He told me a story about when he was 15 and had a major growth spurt; he thought he was a little badass and talked back to her. So, she grabbed him by the ears, pulled him in close, and bit him across the nose. He said he never talked back to her again.

In high school, he started partying, drinking, and smoking weed – nothing that sounded out of the ordinary for a kid dealing with childhood trauma. He was very open about telling us everything he did in his youth, partially to scare us away from making the same mistakes he did. At some point in his early 20s, while drinking, he tried opening a beer bottle by raking it against a tree, and it broke, severely cutting one of his fingers. This injury permanently caused it to not fully close into his hand. He would tell us this story at any chance he got to deter us from drinking.

Sometime in his early 20s, he found God and decided to change his life. I don't know a lot about this time in his life. He owned a construction company and a condo in San Antonio. He started going to church and gave up his business and condo. The story from then is when he met my mom at age 26.

My mom was born to a family of all girls in San Antonio, Texas. She was the fifth of seven girls living in a small house raised by a mostly single mother named Teresa. My mom's father was shot and killed when she was four years old, so her uncle Alvin was the only male role model in her life. She was a shy girl and didn't venture into partying or anything like that in her teenage years. She got a job out of high school working at a bank and traveled a little. She believed in God and went to church regularly. She still lived at home with her mom and younger sister until she met my dad when she was 32. This is when things started to get interesting.

My parents met each other and then got married in five days. Yes, I'll repeat, five days! They met at church on a Sunday and got married on Friday! Talk about feeling a vibe. From what I've heard, God just brought them together, and they knew it was meant to be. Try telling that to her family, though; they were skeptical but supportive of my mom's happiness. Shortly after getting married, God called them to travel and live by faith. So my mom quit her job of 10 years, and they packed up the vehicle and hit the road, leaving family, friends, and their whole lives behind. I don't think they had a plan; my dad lets God or the voice in his head lead him to every decision he makes, as you will see throughout my story.

After marriage and hitting the road, of course, the next step is to bring children into this world. My mom was pregnant with my older sister Rachel, and my dad decided he didn't believe in doctors or the medical system anymore because God would care for everything. I think he may have read some books or asked a few people about home births, but his mind was set on it – no meds for my mom, just pop out a baby the old-fashioned way and then onto the next one. Unfortunately, it didn't go as planned. After several hours of labor at home (or their temporary home in Kansas City, Missouri), they had to call an ambulance and move the birth to the hospital, where finally Rachel Renee Pierson was born on March 10, 1991.

Because she was born in a hospital, she got a little piece of paper called a birth certificate. It can be helpful if you want a normal life as an American citizen. Still, you have to go a couple more steps after leaving the hospital with a newborn to get them a Social Security number for proper identification in the future. However, my parents, or rather my dad, decided not to do that. He wanted us to be "off the grid" because he no longer trusted the government. According to him, God wanted his children to answer only to him and to God. No earthly institution would have a record of his children. This was one of the first things that led to my life being the way it was.

After Rachel was born, we traveled around some more, and my mom was pregnant again, this time with me. Somehow, we ended up staying at a friend's property in a forested area in Tiller, Oregon. This time, they could stick to their plan of no medical assistance. Throughout the pregnancy, there were no checkups, no sonograms, or knowing the baby's sex before birth. But of course, my dad said he felt God was telling him that it would be a boy and kept hearing a name in his head that he didn't know what it was. It just so happened that the couple we were staying with knew some Hebrew. The husband, Stan, was studying Hebrew, and my dad asked Stan about the name God was putting in his thoughts. It was something like "yetsock" or "yetark" or "yetzack," and Stan told him the name "Yitzchak," which was Hebrew for Isaac and meant God's laughter. My father loved it and decided that would be my name even before I was born.

Stan was Polish, and his full name was Stanislaus Petrowski, so that's how I got my middle name: Yitzchak Stanislous Pierson. When the time came for my delivery, we were staying in a cabover camper truck. For those of you who don't know what that is, it's a camper shell that you put in the bed of a pickup truck, essentially allowing you to live in the bed of your truck. And that's where I was born. My mom squatted in the bed of the truck and out popped little ol' me. It was too small to lay down and deliver me. She did this with no pain meds, just all-natural. I was born on October 16, 1992.

Immediately after I was born, my dad decided to hit the road again, not even giving my mom time to recover from giving birth and caring for my sister, who was under two years old. We packed up and left two days after my birth.

We traveled to Montana and spent a few years there. I have my first memories there. It might be a mixture of seeing pictures and hearing stories, but I remember some fun times playing in the snow and being around horses. We stayed with or around an older couple that had a ranch, and my dad worked for them. He grew up watching John Wayne movies and dreaming of the cowboy life. Punk and Mel were kind and tough old-school people, and my dad looked at Punk as a father figure and mentor.

My next two sisters were born in Montana: Moriah on December 15, 1994, and Abigail on June 24, 1995. There was a lot that happened in Montana, and I don't know all the details, but there is an ongoing pattern of my dad befriending people, telling them all the things they were doing wrong in their lives, and then trying to get them to follow him and listen to what he hears from God on how they should be disciplined and correct their sins. Sometimes, people listened to him for a little bit, but there was always a breaking point where they realized they didn't have to listen anymore.

In one of those cases, it resulted in people burning down our house while we were out of the state, so we were essentially driven out of that group of people my dad had befriended. The other significant thing that happened in Montana was my parents meeting Paul and Susan, who were also believers traveling the country. When my dad befriended them, the group expanded, and Paul and Susan decided to travel with us. They believed in my dad, and his calling like no one else had before.

Paul and Susan had one daughter when we first met them; her name was Ally, and she was the same age as me. My dad started his process of influencing them to listen to God through him. So, when they had their second child, Samuel, he was born at home, just like all of us had been – no hospitals, no medications, and no birth certificates or Social Security numbers. I don't know why they thought this was a good idea, but I had no say in the matter.

After traveling together, they decided to return to Texas and settle down. My great-uncle Alvin had five acres in Fischer, Texas, and he let us rent it from him. Paul and Susan parked their travel camper on the property and lived there with us. My dad and Paul started a construction company, which marked the beginning of most of my memories. I was about 4 or 5 years old at this time, and life was still fun. It was cool living in the country, having sheep and chickens, playing outside, and learning new things.

At this house, my youngest sister, Ana, was born on November 8, 1997. At this point in the story, all of us kids were still too young to know that we were any different from other children. We were homeschooled, but we weren't aware of how different our lives were. I knew about God, and I probably prayed and loved God because that's what I was told to do. I remember my dad starting his own church at some point around this time, and he was the pastor, but it didn't last long, and I don't know the reason why.

My dad would go to work, and my mom would stay home, cook, clean, and take care of five kids. It was a very traditional setup where the man was the head of the household and made all the decisions, and the woman was submissive, taking care of the husband and doing what he said. But at some point, my dad started working longer hours and building a relationship with a woman named Denise. As is often the case, when a husband starts staying late and telling his wife there's nothing to worry about, my dad was cheating on my mom, and he soon moved out of the house, leaving my mom for Denise. I think I was seven years old at this point. What I do know is that I was a skinny little kid before the divorce, and like with all childhood trauma, kids find ways to cope. I guess mine was food because I became a chubby kid over the next few years.

Before the divorce, I have memories of the punishments and disciplines we had. I couldn't wear sleeveless shirts or camouflage because of the "macho spirit" my dad believed would take me over. My sisters were not allowed to wear sleeveless shirts or tank tops, and they had to wear long skirts, T-shirts, and shorts that went below their knees, similar to the style of the Amish.

We were meant to wear modest clothes and not really show ourselves, especially my sisters. He believed in the spiritual realm. My dad always talked about good and evil, angels and demons, and that was part of our everyday life as I got older.

I was about seven or eight years old when my parents split up for the first time, and I had a new stepmom figure and a stepsister. We got a little bit more freedom because there were two households, and my dad was marrying somebody else who didn't have the same restrictions that he had. So, it was interesting going back and forth between the households.

My dad was still running the construction company, and my mom lived in a separate household. She lived in Canyon Lake, Texas, and we would go out there and spend the weekends with her. The rest of the time, we would spend with my dad and do our homeschooling in the back room of the construction office.

I remember cheating a lot on my schoolwork and hiding it, like hiding it behind the mirror in the bathroom and just saying that it had gone missing. Looking back on this, I know they knew I was lying, but as a kid, I thought I was smart. Being homeschooled in the back office of a construction company, being in that environment was definitely different from most children's upbringing. We didn't really go out or hang out with any other kids. By this time, Paul and Susan had three children, and there were five of us in our family. So, all of us kids were in the back office, hanging out there. It was weird, though, because there was an elementary school behind the office in Wimberley, Texas, and we got to see kids playing in the playground, but we never really got to do that.

My dad and his fiancée, Denise – they never actually got married but lived together – didn't last very long. They split up after probably a year or two together.

After that, we moved to San Marcos and rented a house. Because my dad was a business owner, we would stay with him during the week because My mom was working a 9 to 5 job Monday-Friday for a title company as a receptionist.

My dad couldn't stay single for long. He had Susan, who was basically his secretary/life assistant, track down a woman he had dated back in his early 20s. He reconnected with Renee, and they picked up where they left off and got married very quickly. She had three children from a previous marriage, so we're still living in San Marcos, and I have three other step-siblings: two girls and a boy. Seeing how they lived and the fact they didn't have restrictions like us was very eye-opening; we realized how different we were being raised compared to other people.

Those views into the outside world probably started my journey to questioning my existence and my place in the world.

They were married for about six months before they got divorced. My dad had a way of meeting a girl and believing she was his "soulmate," and then shortly after, she would see how crazy he was, and it would be over.

Sometime after the divorce, my dad bought seven acres in Martindale, Texas, with a pond. So, we moved out there. My mom was still living in Canyon Lake, and we were with my dad out at the seven acres in Martindale, Texas.

My parents got back together after my dad's other relationships ended; my dad was still the head of the household, and my mom still did whatever he said. She quit working at the title company and started working with him in our businesses. Around that point, I was probably turning 10 years old. We would drive through our town in San Marcos because my dad had his businesses in Wimberley, and we lived in Martindale. To get to and from the businesses, you had to drive through San Marcos, the biggest city of the three.

One time, while driving through San Marcos, we saw somebody set up at a gas station selling rustic furniture, pottery, and wrought iron. My dad stopped and started talking to the guy. My dad was always very talkative and charming, and people really liked him when they first met him. He would have long conversations, and we kids would be standing there just waiting quietly. We knew not to talk or interrupt; we would just be still and listen. So, I got really good at listening when I was young.

He started talking to this guy and learning about the business of furniture, pottery, and wrought iron. He decided it was something that he wanted to get into. So, he went into business with this guy named Jody, who was already selling that type of furniture. Jody had a cargo trailer that he would load up with furniture, unload it at the beginning of the day to display it for sale, and then pack it all up at the end of the day.

And so, that was my first real memory of doing work. I mean, I had fed the animals and cleaned the house and helped out with stuff occasionally, but this was when my dad saw the opportunity to use his kids for free labor. I'm sure he didn't really think that consciously, but I often wonder. We started buying the furniture ourselves from wholesalers, and then we would unload the trailer and set it up to display and sell with Jody. I was 10, and my older sister, Rachel, was probably 12. We were unloading large armoires, entertainment centers, dressers, chest of drawers, and nightstands. It just started out as a weekend thing – Saturdays and

Sundays. We would get to this empty concrete pad in our town, right next to an Arby's. It used to be a drive-through banking station that had been torn down. So, we would back up the trailer, unload the furniture, set it all up nicely to display, and then we would be little salespeople. That was our first introduction to talking to people we didn't know, selling them furniture, pottery, and wrought iron. Occasionally, he'd throw us $20 or something, but overall, we wouldn't get paid for this. My dad said, "Food on the table and a roof over our heads was payment enough."

What started out as just an every Saturday and Sunday thing turned into Thursday, Friday, Saturday, and Sunday—it just became normal. We would do school during the week at home with my mom. She would help us as much as she could and then be there on the weekends with us. We then opened a physical store at the same location where the construction company was and started selling retail out of the construction office. We ended up growing that business and having two locations while still setting up on the side of the road. We decided to make more connections with the wholesalers to buy more in bulk and get better prices, and they were in Laredo. So, we would go down to Laredo, Texas, to meet with the wholesalers, and one thing led to another. We had multiple large trailers. We would fill them up with pottery, wrought iron, and furniture and return to San Marcos to sell them at our stores. This went on for two or three years, working on weekends and during the week, working more and more.

At the same time, we had seven acres in Martindale, Texas, and my dad decided to start getting more animals and have a farm/ranch. So we bought horses, goats, and chickens and started accumulating animals. So, on top of selling furniture, I had to take care of animals at home and go back and forth to Laredo. Eventually, my dad made relationships in Laredo and rented a duplex because it was more convenient than renting hotels when we would go down there for about a month at a time. We actually made a deal to work with one of the wholesale wrought iron and pottery guys to get better prices on our products and be able to buy more in bulk to bring back up to sell in our stores. But my dad had a habit of burning bridges with people, so that ended eventually.

For a while, when I was 13, I was working seven days a week in the pottery and wrought iron yard, living in Laredo. That's really when I quit school altogether. When I was in the seventh grade, around 13 years old, I just didn't see the point in doing school when I had to work so much.

My dad didn't put a lot of value on academic education. We were getting our homeschool books from a Christian publication called Alpha and Omega, and the subjects that we studied were history, language, science, math, and Bible, which focused on biblical stories. My dad didn't really object to me stopping school; he just didn't say anything about it. I was working so much and making money for the family that school just went out the window.

After we stopped going to Laredo when my dad burned his bridge with the wholesaler down there, we would make connections to have more products brought up to us. I remember we had a 54-foot semi-trailer full of pottery stacked from the floor to the ceiling. They used feed bags to pad the pottery so that it wouldn't break in transit. My sisters, the other three children from our group, and I unloaded that whole trailer of pottery. It was very heavy for all of us, and we were completely covered in clay chalk residue colors from all the different potteries. It took us about eight hours to unload it all.

Those are some of my childhood memories of working at an early age. After that, we still worked in the furniture and pottery and wrought iron business, setting stuff up on the side of the road. We went more into farming and agriculture. The furniture business was running more on its own with the different people we had involved taking care of everything. So, my dad decided to get more involved in farming and having horses. He believed he would be a horse whisperer and train horses.

My sisters and I told him we wanted a horse to ride, and he bought an unbroken mare and a foal that we couldn't ride. He just started buying more and more horses, to the point where we had probably 20 horses before we finally got one that we could ride. We also got cows, and at one point, we had 50 head of cows. My dad decided we needed to buy a larger piece of land, so we bought 21 acres out in Kingsbury, Texas, which was about 20 minutes away from our 7 acres in Martindale. We started driving out there probably five days a week or more.

It was a piece of land with a barbed wire fence and a small shed on it, so we had to start working on the fences and putting up structures and water lines. That's what my sister and I did. I was 14 or 15 years old, working on a farm and building a ranch from the ground up every day while still working the furniture business on the weekends. My sister and I built barns, sheds, fences, and gates. We bought a tractor, and I learned how to plow the fields and do everything you would do on a farm. We had horses, cows, goats, chickens, dogs, pigs and donkeys.

I remember one time we had bought some wild donkeys, and I had to go into a pen to try and catch them. I got a lasso around one of their heads and got my arm around it to try and catch it. It bent down and bit my foot through my boot, leaving a big bruise. Also, during my time training horses, I got my first black eye from getting bucked off a horse when I was 15 or 16 in the round pen while trying to train it. I got back up on horses afterward, but I never really liked riding horses after that.

So we had the farm at this point, the furniture business, and the construction company. In between, my dad always had different projects he would start. We had an advertising magazine called the Countywide Shoppers Guide that would go out to several cities. So, we would deliver that magazine in our "free time," driving around the different cities, going into businesses, and leaving the magazines there.

I started working in our construction company full-time when I was probably 16; I went to work with Paul and his son, Samuel, who was younger than me. We were the full construction crew, and I would stay with Paul and Susan and work on different construction jobs for weeks at a time. We did a five-week job in Austin, Texas, just me, Paul, and Samuel, and we stayed at the house we were working on. I remember painting the whole exterior of a three-story house, power washing, peeling the paint off, and then repainting the whole outside and inside of the house. It was definitely not something I wanted to do, but not having a birth certificate, social security number, or any other options to go out into the real world and get a job that I got to choose, that's what I had to do. I'm grateful for it now because I have a really good work ethic, and I know a lot about a lot of things from everything that I was forced to do when I was younger.

What I remember most about growing up was that life was always hard, and it was always a bleak future with no options. When he bought the 21 Acres, my dad wanted us all to grow up and have people marry into our group and live on the same property, like a compound. So, dating was never an option for me growing up, either. We were very sheltered, not attending school or meeting any other girls or guys. He simply wanted us to meet people who joined our church with the expectation that they would marry into the group.

When I was younger, before I started working in construction, I remember he would preach at different congregations while we had the church and all of these businesses. And at that point, he started getting more followers who would help us in the different businesses. At one point, he went up to speak in Dallas and met a young man around 21 years old who had just gotten out of jail. He was searching for more and found God while in jail. He liked what my dad said when he was preaching and started talking to my dad. Then he came down from Dallas to visit us, and he brought his sister and her fiancé to listen to my dad and to learn from him. They all ended up moving down here and giving up their entire lives in Dallas to live with us, work with us, and devote themselves to God and to what my dad told them to do.

After that, we had a few more people come. My dad had his online ministries as well as our brick-and-mortar church. He did his Sunday sermons and then had newsletters and weekly recordings of his sermons that he would put out.

Some people from South Dakota also started interacting with him. They believed in him so much that when the wife got pneumonia and ended up in the hospital, they incurred a lot of financial debt. My dad convinced them, through God, that they should sell everything and turn over all the money to him so that the medical system couldn't come after them for their debts. So, they did just that. They sold their properties, liquidated all their assets, and gave my dad all the money. Consequently, they moved here and dedicated their lives to God and my dad.

Another person named Rick, who was a devoted Y2K believer and doomsday prepper, also joined us. He gave up everything he had prepped and lived with us. All of these people lived in our house at one time or another. I remember Rick staying in my room. He was an older computer guy and very analytical, in his 60s. However, all of these people willingly gave up their whole lives to listen to what my dad said, including what they ate, drank, wore, and even their sexual activities. They gave up their freedoms, which I found very interesting as a child. I thought these people were crazy because my sisters and I had no option. Without birth certificates or social security numbers, we had nowhere to go, and we couldn't leave. So, we had to listen and stay there, doing what we were told. Witnessing all these adults doing that was quite baffling.

Between both of our families and all the people who had come to join and those who would show up at church, we had about 30 to 40 members in the congregation. However, my dad would push people to their limits until they broke.

Some people were put on fasting restrictions, leading to significant weight loss. We had various disciplines like fasting meals or certain meal restrictions, such as going on a water-only fast or eating only plain, cooked pinto beans without seasoning. My dad was very Old Testament Biblical in the sense of judgment, punishments, and disciplines that he imposed on all of us, but mostly his children and followers.

We, as kids, would get spanked as a form of discipline, although it wasn't really physical abuse or beatings. If we got into trouble, we were spanked. We also had other disciplinary measures like being confined to our rooms or being "grounded." Our grounding, however, didn't resemble the typical worldly notion of grounding, as we never went to see friends or had any social life. So, it wasn't the same as grounding in the typical sense.

Being an adult, I sometimes talk about the stories from my childhood, not realizing that it wasn't everybody else's childhood. I remember at one point, my older sister, Rachel, was going through a phase or something. I'm sure it was a result of the way that we were raised. She was lying a lot and blaming things on me. At one point, she took crayons and colored all over one of the walls on one of the outbuildings and said it was me, and I couldn't stop laughing when I was questioned.

When I would lie, I would laugh. And I was laughing because I was saying I didn't do it, but I continued to laugh, and they didn't believe me. So, I kept getting punished. And it went on for, I don't know, a couple of months of her doing things, breaking the screen door, tearing the screen, and then blaming it on me. I remember one time we were in Walmart, and when we got back in the car, my sister pointed out that I had a pack of M&Ms next to me. I had no idea how they got there, but they were sitting there. She said that I had stolen them. And I remember my dad not believing me. I was saying I didn't do it, but I was smiling. And so he made me go back into Walmart and return them, telling the cashier that I had taken the M&Ms and that I was sorry. To make things worse, we had gotten ice cream (we rarely ever got ice cream), but I got my ice cream taken away because of that.

One of the ways that she finally got caught was by putting toothpaste and Comet cleaner all over the bathroom floor and trying to blame it on me. My parents realized it wasn't me because I had been tied to a chair in the living room as a punishment for something else I had done or something else she had accused me of doing.

I didn't realize until I was older that being tied to a chair in the living room as punishment was the most abnormal part of that story. However, receiving such unusual punishments was just part of life for me, and I didn't know any different at the time.

Another part of my childhood was never going to a doctor for anything, as we didn't believe in the medical system. This made my dad very fearful, ensuring that we didn't do things that could harm us, as he dreaded social services getting involved if we ever needed to go to the hospital. This fear stemmed from our lack of birth certificates or social security numbers, not attending school, and not seeing doctors. I can't recall any of us ever going to the hospital or doctor for anything except for occasional visits to the dentist or chiropractor. We had no vaccines, shots, or antibiotics. My dad only allowed dental and chiropractic care because he had back problems after being run over by a cow, and he needed us to drive him around, which I started doing at the age of 10. We had to be extremely careful not to hurt him or his back. Sometimes, we even had to carry a wooden step stool around in the vehicle to help him get in and out of the vehicle. He never believed he would get better and preferred us to serve him hand and foot. He considered himself the head of the group and congregation, and we were meant to serve him.

I remember at one point, my mom got bitten by a brown recluse spider, and we had to pray about everything before deciding what to do. My dad made us pray, and he made her pray about going to the doctor for it. We waited, but her condition worsened as the spider bite began eating away at the flesh on her leg. So, she eventually went to the doctor for treatment and antibiotics. Other than that, I can't remember any of us ever going to the hospital or doctor for anything else.

Not going to public school formed many of my self-limiting beliefs. I believe that not being educated and thinking that I wasn't as smart as others due to my seventh-grade education made me self-conscious and hindered me from pursuing more ambitious goals in life. For most of my upbringing, I worked in manual labor jobs, such as construction, newspaper stuffing, furniture, pottery, and wrought iron businesses, and farming. All of these experiences contributed to my self-limiting belief that I couldn't achieve anything beyond manual labor.

From the way I was raised, I felt like I had no options. College was never an option, and my childhood seemed very bleak. It wasn't until I was about 16 that I began to see a future outside of working for my dad and living my life for him instead of living my own life. Growing up, I had no childhood or friendships and struggled with social anxiety. We were molded to be very compliant and had to hide our true selves around my dad. When it was just us kids, we could be ourselves, but we had to censor ourselves around my mom because she would sometimes report back to my dad. While my sisters and I got along quite well, we learned to hide our true selves around my dad, unable to be authentic.

CHAPTER 2

THE "NORMAL" LIFE

Being isolated from mainstream society and lacking access to public schools and medical care had a significant impact on my worldview. I didn't know what the real world was like. I thought that if I could just get out of this situation, I could have a normal life. The only dream I had as a child was to lead a normal life, get a job, take care of myself, and have my own place and my own car. It was a simple life that I dreamed of. However, it was never an option for me due to not "existing" or being a "ghost child." It wasn't until I was 15 years old that my older sister Rachel ran away from home. My younger sisters and I pooled our money to help her escape, hoping she would eventually come back and save us. She hitchhiked to Houston but soon realized that, without a Social Security Number, she couldn't take care of herself. So, she had to call my dad, and he went to Houston to pick her up.

After they returned, he sat us down, which was a common occurrence in our lives. These talks were often more challenging than physical punishments, as they would go on for hours. During these talks, he would try to impose his beliefs on us, and we had to sit and listen until any individuality or dissenting opinions we had were minimized or taken away. If we expressed our own opinions, he would continue talking to us until we "admitted" that we were wrong. Eventually, we realized that he would never change or see things from our perspective.

As a result, we became skilled at concealing our true selves and telling him what he wanted to hear to expedite the end of these conversations. He would typically position himself on his bed or a couch, making us sit on the floor below him, reinforcing his belief that he was our superior and the head of the household. These talks were mentally draining, and there was more mental and verbal abuse than physical abuse.

When my sister ran away and returned, we endured days of talks as a punishment. Rachel was required to cut her long red hair short. My sister Moriah, the middle sister, was most like my dad in terms of unwavering beliefs. She aspired to be an actress and was skilled at feigning emotions to get her way. However, my dad viewed her as the most rebellious, and she remained unchanged after the running-away incident.

My dad was an adulterous womanizer who believed himself to be a Casanova. He had affairs and kept them hidden from my mom. Even when we lived in Laredo part-time, my dad was dating other women and using dating websites. He would tell us kids about some of it and make us keep it a secret from my mom, making us accomplices. As a result, Moriah was aware of all these affairs. Despite my dad's belief that we weren't very intelligent, we were naturally curious and had no other activities except snooping and playing detective. We did everything we could to uncover secrets and hidden truths.

My dad forced my mom to move out of the house so that he could spend more time with the woman he was seeing in our group. My mom moved to San Marcos and rented a house, which my dad paid for. She continued working for my dad in our businesses: furniture, pottery, and wrought iron. My dad believed Moriah was becoming more and more rebellious, so he sent her to live with my mom as punishment. This turned out to be a pivotal moment because it gave Moriah more freedom to grow as a person, live with my mom without my dad's constant supervision, and expose my dad's true nature.

We were prohibited from using social media, but Moriah created Myspace and Facebook accounts, allowing her to meet people in San Marcos while my mom was at work. Moriah gradually convinced my mom to confront my dad about his actions, shedding light on his behavior. With my mom no longer under my dad's constant watch, she was able to see the truth. This was the turning point that hinted at the possibility of a better future. My mom finally broke free from my dad, emptied the bank account, and gathered as much money as possible to start living independently, which was only $3,000. She found a job at a title company as a receptionist and decided to help us obtain our birth certificates and Social Security numbers. My dad sending Moriah away was the catalyst for us obtaining these vital documents. My mom started by helping Moriah get her documents first.

Getting my birth certificate was the most challenging because my name is Yitzchak Stanislous Pierson, and I was born in Oregon. We didn't have many documents to submit, so obtaining a delayed birth certificate was a complex process involving multiple interactions with the government. Fortunately, the people who owned the property where I was born still lived in Oregon. Stanislaus Petrowski and his wife were able to sign an affidavit and testify in a phone hearing. I remember calling into the court for their testimony to confirm my identity and birthplace. Finally, at the age of 18, I received my birth certificate, followed by obtaining a Social Security number and driver's license. After my mom left and Moriah lived with her, my sister Abigail chose to live with my mom.

My dad couldn't do much about this situation as he feared the involvement of social services and the government. He had to allow Abigail to live with my mom and maintain a cordial relationship. He began providing my mom with a small monthly payment for child support for my sisters living with her. Strangely, they never filed taxes regarding us kids or listed us in the court system during either divorce. They didn't even acknowledge having any children.

I wanted a normal life, and the conventional path was for kids to stay with their parents until they turned 18, regardless of how difficult their lives were. I knew that many children had it worse than I did. So, I consciously decided to remain with my dad until I turned 18, with the intention of learning as much as possible. I resolved to take the positive lessons and leave behind the negative experiences. Working in construction, the furniture and pottery business, and on the ranch, I acquired valuable skills to take into the real world.

That's why I stayed. In the months leading up to my 18th birthday, my dad discovered my plans to leave and tried to convince me to stay through multiple talks. Until that point, he had always been able to persuade us and change our minds. However, I had a girlfriend at that time and had gained access to Myspace when I visited my mom and sisters. I met a girl on Myspace, and I initially wanted my dad to disapprove of our relationship. Surprisingly, he approved but required that we be supervised whenever we were together. Having a girlfriend during my last year with my dad was likely the only reason I stayed that long. If I hadn't had someone to talk to or a connection to the outside world, I probably wouldn't have made it to my 18th birthday.

On the day I turned 18, I moved in with my mom in San Marcos and set goals for myself. My first goal was to obtain my GED, followed by acquiring a vehicle and securing a job. My grandmother on my dad's side had passed away a few years earlier and had a life insurance policy. However, she was aware of my dad's financial habits and chose not to leave the money with him.

Instead, she entrusted it to one of our uncles until we turned 21. The policy was worth $9,000 for each of us five kids. When I turned 18, I approached my uncle to request a portion of the money to buy a vehicle, allowing me to find employment. He granted me $3,750, which I used to purchase a 1992 Ford F-150 truck, my first vehicle. Despite having driven since I was 10 years old, I didn't obtain my driver's license until after turning 18. To study for my GED, I began visiting the public library, marking my first experience in a classroom setting with standardized testing. In our homeschooling, we didn't encounter multiple-choice questions; instead, we had to write out the correct answers, which our parents would then check. Any mistakes had to be corrected.

So when our schoolwork was done, I guess we were technically "A" students. Going into the GED studying, having multiple-choice questions where I just had to block out the one that I thought was correct wasn't too hard. I took a couple of practice tests, and I passed the practice test well. So then I went and took the actual GED test, and I passed above average. The way the GED is scored is you have five subjects, and you need an average score of 450 to pass. The scoring is from 200 to 800. I ended up getting an average score of 598, which surprised me because I only had a 7th-grade education. But I believe we did get a lot more common sense with how we were raised and working in businesses. My dad always showed us the numbers and showed us the budgets and what the companies were making. So, from an early age, I had a good business education when it came to numbers.

Looking back on my childhood and knowing everything that I know now about my dad and the way that he functioned, it made sense to me the first time I heard about narcissistic personality disorder. I looked it up because someone said it sounded like my dad, and it described him perfectly.

Narcissistic personality disorder is a mental health condition in which people have an unreasonably high sense of their importance. They need and seek a lot of attention and want people to admire them. People with this disorder may lack the ability to understand or care about the feelings of others. But behind this mask of extreme confidence, they are not sure of their self-worth and are easily upset by the slightest criticism.

A narcissistic personality disorder causes problems in many areas of life, such as relationships, work, school, or financial matters. People with narcissistic personality disorder may be generally unhappy and disappointed when they're not given the special favors or admiration that they believe they deserve. They may find their relationships troubled and unfulfilling, and other people may not enjoy being around them. Symptoms of narcissistic personality disorder and how severe they are can vary. People with the disorder can:

- Have an unreasonably high sense of self-importance and require constant, excessive admiration.

- Feel that they deserve privileges and special treatment.

- Expect to be recognized as superior even without achievements.

- Make achievements and talents seem bigger than they are.

- Be preoccupied with fantasies about success, power, brilliance, beauty, or the perfect mate.

- Believe they are superior to others and can only spend time with or be understood by equally special people.

- Be critical of and look down on people they feel are not important.

- Expect special favors and expect other people to do what they want without questioning them.

- Take advantage of others to get what they want.

- Have an inability or unwillingness to recognize the needs and feelings of others.

- Be envious of others and believe others envy them.

- Behave in an arrogant way, brag a lot, and come across as conceited.

- Insist on having the best of everything — for instance, the best car or office.

At the same time, people with narcissistic personality disorder have trouble handling anything they view as criticism. They can:

- Become impatient or angry when they don't receive special recognition or treatment.

- Have major problems interacting with others and easily feel slighted.

- React with rage or contempt and try to belittle other people to make themselves appear superior.

- Have difficulty managing their emotions and behavior.

- Experience major problems dealing with stress and adapting to change.

- Withdraw from or avoid situations in which they might fail.

- Feel depressed and moody because they fall short of perfection.

- Have secret feelings of insecurity, shame, humiliation, and fear of being exposed as a failure.

He has all of the symptoms of narcissistic personality disorder. We always thought he was bipolar, which he might also be, but he would never go to a doctor or a psychiatrist because he's actually very smart and knows not to say certain things to certain people. So that goes more hand in hand with narcissistic personality disorder. And then you combine that with religion and him thinking that he hears directly from God; that's when you get people like David Koresh and the Waco incident. Fortunately, it was never that bad for us. We didn't stockpile guns or anything like that, but we had a lot of the same similarities to Mormonism.

I recently read a book called *Educated,* written by Tara Westover, about her upbringing in the Mormon community in the late 80s. There were several similarities between her father in that book and my father. So it's something that I look back on. And I'm grateful for the lessons that I learned. And I don't regret my childhood because I wouldn't be who I am without it. And I don't have any hard feelings towards my dad. He believed that he was doing everything in his power and to the best of his ability. He truly believed that he was doing the right thing in his mind.

Over the years, one of the ways that I've learned to achieve my goals is by breaking them down into smaller, more achievable moves. For example, what are the five moves I need to do to accomplish this one goal, and then even get more granular on each of those five moves? If it still seems too big, then keep going with simplifying each move, or you can use SMART Goals.

The SMART goal framework is a mnemonic used to guide the development of measurable and achievable goals. SMART stands for Specific, Measurable, Achievable, Realistic, and Time-bound. This method ensures that goals are clear, concise, and actionable.

Specific: Goals should be well-defined and clear. This means that the goal is straightforward, emphasizing what you want to accomplish. Avoid vagueness. For instance, instead of saying, "I want to get fit," a specific goal might be, "I want to run a 5K in under 30 minutes."

Measurable: Goals should have criteria for measuring progress. This ensures that you can track your progress and stay motivated. It also helps you determine when the goal has been achieved. Using the previous example, the measure is the ability to run a 5K in under 30 minutes.

Achievable: While goals should be challenging, they should also be realistic and attainable. This concept considers the resources, knowledge, and time available for achieving the goal. Setting goals that are too easy or too challenging can lead to a lack of motivation.

Realistic: Don't set yourself up for failure by setting goals that are too ambitious. Start with small, achievable goals and then gradually increase your goals as you achieve success. For instance, for someone whose primary objective is to enhance cardiovascular health and start a running habit, it is more realistic to run a 5K than a marathon to start with.

Time-bound: Every goal should have a target date, which creates a sense of urgency and a clear timeframe for completion. For our example, a time-bound addition might be "I want to run a 5K in under 30 minutes within the next six months."

The SMART framework is widely used in business, coaching, and personal development settings to provide clarity and direction in goal-setting. It's a structured way to ensure that goals are actionable and aligned with broader objectives.

I was able to accomplish my childhood dream of being normal and having an ordinary life. I got my GED, I got a vehicle, I got a job at 18 working at a manufacturing facility, Thermon Manufacturing. I had an interview. Because of the resume that I was able to produce, working construction, and working all of these different jobs that I had before I turned 18, I was hired and started the job at $12 an hour. I was hired to build these big electrical panels. The company we worked for built large electrical panels for power plants and oil refineries. I started out as more of a grunt, just doing whatever they told me and learning as I went. I was very quiet, but I knew if I worked hard, I would get noticed. If I showed up on time every day, or even early, I would be able to make money and eventually live on my own. That was my next goal. I would live with my mom for a year, and then I would get my own place after I saved up enough money and learned more about how the world worked.

I started working in this manufacturing plant, and my hard work ethic was noticed shortly by a guy in another department in the metal fabrication department named Darryl Wahl. He took me under his wing, brought me over to his department, and got me out of the job that I was doing where I was just being moved around, and he started advocating for me. I was originally hired as a temporary employee. Within three months, I was hired as a full-time employee with benefits, a 401K, and paid time off. I was the youngest person working there at the time and one of the quickest to get hired on as a full-time employee. There were some other employees there that had been Temps for two years and had been let go and then came back and were still Temps. I know some of them were a little upset over the fact that I was younger and had been hired on so quickly. The work ethic that I learned from growing up was paying off, and I was getting noticed.

At this point, I was pretty stable for about a year. I had broken up with the girl that I had been dating when I was 17. Getting out into the real world and having so many more options, the relationship just didn't work out. After that, it was really my first time getting into the dating world and starting to see more girls. So, once I had a job and a car, then girls were my main focus. I started seeing as many girls as I could, and that's the first thing I put my energy toward before I really got into anything else like drinking or smoking.

Being 18 and working in a manufacturing facility with so many older people, alcohol was a big part of life for most of these people. I remember being at the bars at 18 years old and getting offered drinks. I turned them down at that point. I remember my first time smoking weed was actually while I was taking my GED classes at the library. I met a guy there, and he asked if I smoked weed. I lied and said I did. And then he asked if I wanted to go drive around and smoke with him. And so I did. I was smoking out of a pipe and had never smoked out of a pipe before. I didn't know what to do. And he asked me about it. And I was like, "Oh, no, I've only ever smoked joints." And so he showed me how to smoke out of a pipe. I didn't really get high from it. And then, maybe a week or two after that, I tried it again with some other people. I hadn't ever smoked or drank anything growing up, but San Marcos was a college town, and I found out that even some of the people I worked with smoked.

So, I started smoking weed. And then, being the entrepreneurial person I was, I didn't see the point in just smoking weed and paying for it. So, I decided to start selling weed to make a little bit of money and to be able to smoke for free. I then realized that that was a way to make friends and meet people. Smoking was just the thing that everybody did in this town. And so that's how I started meeting more people and getting past my social anxiety. There was a mutual activity that we all did together, and that was getting high. And being the person who always had weed and who sold weed, I got to know a lot more people. I was buying quarter pounds of weed, what we called swag, which was Mexican dirt weed; it wasn't very good stuff. And so I was buying it a quarter pound at a time, selling it, and still working my manufacturing job. I did that from about 18 to 19 years old.

And that's the only way that I knew people; they weren't the best people looking back on it. It wasn't a good crowd that I got into. At a certain point, I was getting calls from people wanting weed in the middle of the night, and I didn't like that. I started buying DRO or hydro. It was a much better weed that was more expensive and would attract a higher-paying clientele, so I started selling that. It also cut back on the sketchy people I'd been dealing with.

I started drinking a little bit, and I got invited to a party. It ended up being in the apartment complex that my mom and I lived in at the time. It was early, probably 10 or 11 o'clock at night, and I tried to be smart with my selling. I would keep the weed in a metal lockbox because I knew that the police had to have a warrant to open it. I'd carry around a backpack with my lockbox in it. And we went to this spring break party in this apartment complex and were getting all set up for it. There was a knock on the door, and somebody opened the door without looking through the peephole to see who it was. It was the police, and there was a bong, a pipe, and a grinder sitting out in plain view. The whole apartment smelled like weed. So that gave the police all the probable cause they needed to come in and search the whole apartment.

I knew the three girls that were living there. Cops came in, searched the whole apartment, and found weed, bongs, pipes, grinders, and baggies; they did one final check, tapped on my backpack, heard the metal box, and wanted to open it and ask what was in it. I told them it was industrial documents because I worked in manufacturing, and it was manufacturing documents.

Of course, the cop didn't believe me and said, "So you're saying I can't open it?"

I said, "Yeah, that's what I'm saying. You can't open it."

So they just said they were going to keep us there all night, And they were going to get a search warrant and get dogs out there if I didn't cooperate. So I decided to cooperate because I didn't want more of my friends to get arrested because of me. I opened it up, and I had an ounce of weed on me, my baggies, and my scale. They asked me why I had baggies and a scale. I told them that I just like to know how much I smoked, so I portioned it out so that *Mindful Metamorphosis* would last me the whole month.

They probably knew I was lying, but they took it a little easier on us because we all cooperated. They took the bongs, pipes, and everything out to the dumpster and broke them all up. And then they arrested four of us. That was my first time getting arrested and being in the back of a cop car and then going to the jail and getting my mug shots and fingerprints taken and being in a cold, bright jail cell. It was definitely an eye-opening experience. I remember there was one guy in there who was all drugged up on bars, which is Xanax, and just had his nose broken and had gotten into a fight. I remember it being super cold, laying there on a stainless steel bench and just thinking about everything my whole childhood, growing up, and everything my dad said, and then getting arrested at 19. Trying to call my mom to get bailed out. It was a very unenjoyable experience. When I got out the next day, I quit smoking cold turkey.

I just knew that I'd have bills to pay and things to deal with. I still had my job at Thermon; they didn't find out about the arrest. I was good at keeping secrets from having to do that so much growing up in the environment that I grew up in.

I had to deal with getting a lawyer and figuring out what would happen to me and how the court system works. It takes a long time before you find anything out. I was charged with possession of marijuana under two ounces.

At that point, I had moved out of my mom's. I got my own place where I had two other roommates, and one of the other roommates sold weed, too. So, I still couldn't get away from it, even though I quit smoking. I was still surrounded by it. Everybody I knew smoked, but a lot of "friends" fell off. People I used to sell to didn't hang out with me anymore. Since I wasn't smoking, a lot of people who I thought were my friends didn't show up or call me anymore. So that was my first experience with seeing how fake people can be, whether they're really your friends or they're just around you for what you have or what they can get from you.

That was probably my first experience with seeing how the people you surround yourself with and the environment that you're in help create your reality. It really makes a big difference. I think it was about seven months later that I started smoking again. I finally got my sentencing, and I was able to get pre-trial diversion and got 1-year probation, 24 hours of community service, and about $1,000 in court fees. After that, I straightened up for a little bit but still would smoke occasionally and still was working, dating, having fun, and enjoying my normal life.

I was overweight; my first introduction to exercise and working out started at 19 years old, forming the habits that would later carry me to success in life. I was 250 pounds at my heaviest because I just smoked weed and ate food all the time. A lot of the people that I hung out with, that's all they did. We'd get together and smoke, get the munchies, and go eat and didn't really do anything active. I decided to start losing weight, so I cut out fast food and soda to start with and just started jogging whenever I could, jogging and walking and then jogging and walking. Around that time, my company was holding a "biggest loser competition" to incentivize employees to lose weight, and I entered the competition.

I decided to cut out drinking. I hired a personal trainer because I had never lifted weights before and didn't want to hurt myself. So I worked out with a personal trainer three times a week for an hour at a time for a whole month so that I could learn the exercises and how to do them properly. As it was getting closer to the end of the biggest loser competition, I was in third place, so I asked my personal trainer how to lose the most weight over the weekend. It was a Friday. I had already been dieting and exercising six or seven days a week. He told me to jog at least four miles every day — Friday, Saturday, and Sunday. I was eating five small meals a day of broccoli, spinach, and tilapia. And on Sunday, he said don't drink any water after noon. That way, you lose all your water weight by Monday morning weigh-ins. Over the weekend, by dedicating myself to doing everything the trainer told me to do, I lost 13 pounds and won the biggest loser competition. I lost 25% of my body weight. I think I went from 250 pounds down to 190 pounds.

But then I would go back to drinking and eating whatever I wanted and put weight back on. I think at my lowest, I got down to 170 pounds. I had done another weight loss competition probably a year or 2 after the biggest loser, with some guys from work where we all just put in $20 a piece to see who could lose the most weight in a month. I went from 205 pounds down to 180 in 30 days. So, learning about exercise and diet and forming habits was my first introduction to seeing how I could change my physical body through small habits and being disciplined.

I got into mountain biking a lot in my early 20s and prioritized health and exercise more. I would go mountain biking with some of the guys I worked with five days a week in San Marcos at these outdoor trails called Purgatory Creek. I ended up doing a 24-hour mountain bike race for my 21st birthday: five guys in a relay-style race on a 10-mile track where we would go out one person at a time. And when that person would come in, the next one would go out. We finished in fourth place out of about 15 teams from all over Texas. I did three laps. My first one was around 5 p.m., and then my next lap was around 10 p.m. And then my final lap was around 3 a.m. This was around October 16th; it was about 40 degrees, cold and rainy. And the trails were all sloshy and muddy by the end of it. It's definitely one of the toughest things I've ever done, but it was a great accomplishment for my 21st birthday. I was in really great shape before getting more into drinking after I turned 21.

My weight loss journey over the years was a yo-yo experience or a roller coaster ride. But it taught me how to be disciplined and accomplish things by setting my mind to it. I was also able to cut out drinking whenever I wanted to do a weight loss competition; having a monetary goal made it easier, too. When I won the biggest loser competition, I got $400 in airline tickets and $200 in hotel gift cards. And when I won the other competition with my coworkers, I won $320. Having a goal at the end of the task made it easier for me to accomplish. I would consider it a short-term sacrifice for the long-term reward. If I could take 30 days of not doing something to know that I was going to get a reward at the end of those 30 days, it would be a lot easier for me to do it.

But, like anything, it depends on the environment you put yourself in and the people you surround yourself with. After I turned 21, exercise was still important to me; I would still work out and be active, but then I would go back to my old habits of drinking and eating whatever I wanted to and slacking off. And a lot of the people that I hung out with outside of work and outside of the mountain biking group did not work out. They didn't do anything other than drink or smoke or party. Spending my 20s in San Marcos, a college town, going out to the bars was just a part of life. I would go see a lot of live music; a lot of my friends were musicians, so that was just part of life, and going to parties was all just part of the lifestyle. My priorities at that time were sex, getting girls, and alcohol. And then drugs came third to that. It just started out with weed. I went to a lot of raves before I was 21. I did some Molly and ecstasy, some Adderall, some things like that.

And then, in San Marcos, with drinking and partying, cocaine came into the picture at a certain point in my early 20s. I remember the first time I was around it. I never did it. But the more you're around something, the more normal it becomes, the more normal it seems when everybody you know is doing it. It doesn't seem like it's such a bad thing. So, the first time I ever did it, I still remember being in an apartment, staying up all night. I didn't really see what the big deal was. It wasn't like I was addicted. It just was something that was there that was offered. I didn't pay for it. I was just doing it because everybody else was doing it. And that's something I've learned over the years: addiction doesn't necessarily just happen from first-time use; it's from the associations that you have and the people that you're around. If it's normal and that's what everybody's doing, then it seems like it's something that's not that big of a deal. When I started doing it more regularly, it was just a small baggie with friends on a weekend when we were really drunk; somebody would get it, and we just split it.

39

After that, it became a more frequent occurrence, happening every weekend or at the start of each weekend. We couldn't go out drinking with my group of friends without cocaine being present or being a part of our activities. The same applied to alcohol in general. Looking back, it was similar to when I used to smoke. There was a time when I was smoking every day, and I didn't want to be constantly smoking, but that's what everyone I hung out with did. Wherever we went, whatever activity we engaged in, we had to smoke first. Eventually, I managed to break that smoking habit.

However, it morphed into a drinking habit. Everywhere we went, every event we attended, alcohol took center stage. We rarely went anywhere if alcohol wasn't available. I seldom drank alone; I was more of a social drinker, enjoying the company of my friends. I also appreciated how alcohol made me more outgoing and sociable, especially since I struggled with social anxiety. Alcohol boosted my confidence and removed the filter between my brain and my mouth.

I would say and do outrageous things, not always presenting the best version of myself. I wanted to be as carefree and fun-loving as some of my other friends, so I started doing things I would never consider when sober. I did have friends who were even more reckless than me, and I used that as a justification, thinking, *I'm not as crazy as that person when I drink.* I've heard stories about the things I did, and they're not experiences I'd want to relive.

I did have friends who could drink socially without going overboard. Unfortunately, I was never the type to have just one beer. If I was going out, I intended to get drunk and have a good time. However, this lack of moderation led to a lack of responsibility. Once I reached a certain level of drunkenness, I would stop making responsible choices. This eventually led to a DWI when I was 23. It happened after leaving my best friend's party in Lockhart. I had stopped drinking around 11 p.m. because I was with a couple of girls I wanted to impress, so I tried to sober up. The drive back to my house in San Marcos was about 20 minutes, but I got pulled over at a stoplight. I wasn't extremely drunk at that moment, but it was 2 o'clock in the morning, and I ended up getting arrested and spending the night in jail.

More people in my social circle were getting DWIs. At that point, I probably knew about 10 people with DWIs, including some coworkers from my manufacturing job. Many of them were heavy drinkers. Thankfully, my boss, Darryl, had been sober for about 20 years, and he set a good example. However, I still didn't listen to the people around me. I worked with a guy who had three DWIs, even after going to rehab as a court-ordered mandate. Despite my mom and sisters trying to talk to me about improving my drinking and driving habits, I didn't listen. Following my DWI, I had to deal with lawyer fees as I tried to keep it under wraps so that not everyone at work would find out, fearing the potential job consequences.

Through the years, I've learned that no matter how many times people try to advise you or how many times you hear the truth and know what you need to change, it ultimately comes down to your own desire to make that change. No one else can do it for you, no matter how much they try to help. If someone isn't willing to help themselves, there comes a point where you must let them make their mistakes and move on. Continuously trying to help them when they don't put in any effort becomes enabling.

My behavior didn't change significantly after the DWI incident. I recall getting out of jail the next morning, retrieving my truck from the impound lot, and immediately going to a taco place bar with my friend to drink and reflect on the situation. I fulfilled my legal obligations, paid my lawyer, and fortunately had my first arrest expunged, so this was legally considered my first offense. It took about a year or two before I received sentencing, but I managed to secure pretrial adjudication (pretrial diversion). I was sentenced to one year of probation, had to pay court fees, attend DWI classes, perform 24 hours of community service, and attend some AA meetings. I had previously attended an AA meeting for my first arrest, even though it was related to a marijuana charge. It wasn't something I felt was necessary. While I acknowledge that AA helps many people, my upbringing made it difficult for me to place my faith in a higher power like God.

I understood that if I wanted to change, I had to be the one to make the choices to transform my life. So, the second time around, I completed all the required tasks for the DWI case but continued drinking. I remember attending one of my probation meetings after drinking the night before and occasionally using cocaine. I knew it would take a day or two to clear my system, so I would stop using a day or two before scheduled drug tests. My social circle consisted of people dealing with various legal issues, so it felt like a normal part of our lives. I didn't see the need to change.

I had been employed in manufacturing for five years, and I wanted to advance or earn more money. Unfortunately, my job didn't offer much room for growth or career development. In manufacturing, you often find people who work overtime just to make ends meet, and it's not a high-paying profession. When I started at 18, my hourly wage was $12, and I was considered a good employee, receiving a $1.17 raise within the first three months, an uncommon achievement at my workplace. Some individuals worked as temporary employees for years before getting permanent positions.

Despite my partying, I prioritized my job and punctuality, which meant I didn't drink during the week and saved it for the weekends. Fridays and Saturdays were dedicated to drinking, and on Sundays, I played in a pool league, which introduced Sunday drinking into the mix. Occasionally, I would call in sick on Mondays due to hangovers, a practice common among my coworkers. Monday was the day for people to call in due to weekend partying; it was an unspoken norm.

Over the years, I received a few raises. But after five years, I wanted to make a change; I needed another job unless I received a significant pay increase. Eventually, they offered an additional dollar per hour and full benefits, including a 401k and dental and medical coverage. I thought, *For my age, I have a good job.* I didn't know what else I wanted to do in life, so I decided to continue working there. After 10 years, 10 months, and 24 days (but who's counting, right?) at that job, I began to notice a pattern: their sole focus was to extract maximum work for minimum pay. I fell right in line with this mentality of doing what everyone else was doing at the job and lowered my standards. Initially, I excelled and was recognized as Employee of the Month and Employee of the Quarter, receiving praise and raises.

However, as new management came in, there were no raises for a couple of years. Many coworkers became negative and bitter about their jobs. Some had been there so long that they couldn't imagine starting over elsewhere or were too comfortable in the routine and mediocrity. They were either nearing retirement or reluctant to embrace change. This negativity began to affect me as well. I stopped pushing myself and did the bare minimum. I would complete my tasks and then goof off as much as possible. Many of us adopted the mentality that if we weren't paid enough, we would do the least amount of work necessary. We would arrive early and do nothing for the first 15 to 20 minutes before starting our tasks, milking the clock to accumulate overtime without management noticing.

I did have a great supervisor, Darryl; he was a good mentor to me. He'd give me money out of his own pocket anytime I needed it, or if I'd go on vacation, he'd give me a little money to spend. He was a great guy, loved to give people a hard time, and was a bit of an asshole at times. Surprisingly, I loved working with him. Many people would say, "I don't know how you work with him," but considering my upbringing and dealing with my dad, working with Darryl felt like a piece of cake. He's a genuinely caring person underneath his tough exterior, and I truly appreciated having him in my life during the years I worked there.

However, there were other people at the company who were negative every morning right from the moment they started their work day. They brought a negative attitude, creating a hostile work environment. Many departments seemed to work against each other, with each trying to shift the workload onto the next department, causing undue pressure on them. This lack of teamwork was quite apparent.

As I've grown older, I've learned more about leadership. Unfortunately, good leadership in manufacturing facilities or large companies is often scarce because they prioritize the bottom line. Nevertheless, this experience taught me valuable lessons, particularly how I tended to conform to the expectations around me, doing no more than what was required.

I distinctly remember a time when I was making around $14 an hour, and I stumbled upon another guy's paycheck on the ground. I saw that he was making about $15 an hour for simply sitting at a table and assembling small wire pieces. My job as a CNC machine operator involved metal fabrication, blueprint reading, re-engineering, custom panel fabrication, crane operation, and forklift driving. I was doing significantly more, yet this guy earned more than me just because of his seniority. It frustrated me to see people slacking off and being lazy while earning the same or even higher pay than me. This ongoing disparity in pay became one of the things that increasingly bothered me over the years – not being compensated according to what I believed I was worth.

I always said I would leave if I ever became unhappy there. It's one of those situations where you get trapped in a job you despise, constantly expressing your desire to leave but never actually doing so because it's comfortable and predictable. I knew I could come in, clock in my hours, do the bare minimum, clock out, and not worry about anything. I could go about my life, enjoy my weekends, and even call in sick without fear of losing my job. Many of my acquaintances followed a similar pattern, working during the week and eagerly waiting for the weekend to party — the "weekend warrior" mentality. It was a repetitive cycle, and after a while, I got really tired of it. I yearned for more out of life because the "normal" life I had always desired didn't live up to my expectations.

During this period, I stumbled upon a book that profoundly impacted me, *The Myth of Normal* by Gabor Maté. In the book, Dr. Maté, a renowned physician and author, challenged society's conventional understanding of "normal." He questioned how contemporary culture often stigmatizes or categorizes what is considered "abnormal" or "pathological" without considering the broader environmental and societal factors at play.

Maté's book explored several key themes:

1. *Definition of Normal*: Maté questioned the societal standards defining "normal" behavior and suggested that many behaviors

deemed "abnormal" are natural responses to environmental or stress-related factors.

2. *Trauma and Its Effects*: He emphasized the profound impact of trauma, particularly early childhood trauma, on both mental and physical health, linking conditions like addiction and depression to unresolved trauma.

3. *Environment and Mental Health*: Maté argued that societal structures, such as the education system and workplace, can contribute to mental health issues. The fast-paced nature of modern life, coupled with a lack of genuine human connection, can harm our well-being.

4. *Holistic Approach to Treatment*: Instead of solely medicating symptoms, Maté advocated for a holistic approach to mental health that considers a person's entire life experience, including physical health, emotional well-being, and social environment.

5. *Empathy and Connection*: He stressed the importance of empathy and genuine human connection in the healing process, often more effective than clinical interventions.

6. *Critique of the Medical Model*: Maté criticized the prevailing medical model of mental health, which often focuses on categorizing and medicating symptoms instead of addressing root causes.

In essence, "The Myth of Normal" encouraged a deeper understanding and a more compassionate approach to mental health, emphasizing the interconnectedness of individual well-being with societal structures and environmental factors.

Around the age of 25, I began searching for more meaning in my life. A friend from my pool league introduced me to a different lifestyle. Her boyfriend's family had more wealth than I had ever encountered. We visited Lake Texoma on the Texas/Oklahoma border, where I witnessed a completely different way of life. They had a three-story vacation house with a three-car garage, a beautiful lakefront home, an ATV to reach the boat dock, and an apartment at the dock. Their impressive boat collection included a Cobalt boat, four jet skis, and another ski boat. Her boyfriend's father also owned another boat house at a marina, complete with a three-bedroom apartment and a high-speed cigarette boat (that went 100 miles per hour!). He was a plastic surgeon who loved to ski barefoot.

What struck me most was not just the material possessions but the overall experience and their kindness. While we partied and had a great time, I couldn't help but think about what it would take to achieve a similar lifestyle or provide such experiences to others. It was a wake-up call, prompting me to consider changing my life and pursuing different goals.

It was a glimpse into what my future could be, but with the route I was on, there was no way that was going to be possible. There was no way that I could make enough money working in manufacturing to afford anything like that.

So after I got back from that trip, that's when I really started searching and looking for more out of life, different things to invest in. I thought, *Okay, I've had enough of this. I do not want a normal life. I want an extraordinary life. I want more out of life. I want to be able to give people these experiences that I just had.*

I began by Googling and searching for different things to invest in, side hustles, anything I could think of. I looked into stocks, bonds, and running my own business to figure out what I was good at. Growing up, I had experience in construction, furniture making, pottery, wrought iron work, farming, and ranching. However, I didn't really want to go back to any of those things. I forget how I found it, but real estate investing just kept coming up. In multiple places that I researched, real estate investing was a recurring theme. I started watching YouTube videos and listening to podcasts. The "Bigger Pockets" podcast was one of the first real estate investing podcasts that I listened to. I also started following a guy named Graham Stephan on YouTube, a real estate investor and realtor in California. I learned a lot about how I could invest and what I could invest in.

One advantage I had was good credit. Despite all of my partying and everything I did, I still paid all my bills on time. I had worked really hard because I grew up seeing my dad ruining his credit, taking out all this debt, and borrowing money from people. That was something I never wanted to do.

I learned about buy-and-hold real estate investing, which involves buying properties and holding them as full-time rentals. Then I discovered house hacking, where you buy a house and rent out the rooms and the people you rent to pay for your mortgage. That seemed like an achievable path.

I was still going to keep working in manufacturing, and I was still going to keep doing what I was doing. I just decided, "Okay, I have a job. I have the safety and security of this job. I know what to expect here. I make decent money to pay my bills, and I can save up." I set some goals in place and decided I needed to pay off all my debt and save up money for a down payment on my first house. I started working towards those goals and continually learning.

YouTube was the easiest way for me to learn. I still didn't really read books because of the way I was homeschooled. We were only allowed to read Bible books or the books that my dad had written, and any other books had to be approved by him. So, I never really picked up the habit of reading. We didn't have to do book reports, and because I had quit school at a young age, it wasn't part of my life. So, watching YouTube videos was my introduction to learning. Then I discovered podcasts and went down rabbit holes, exploring different channels and listening to various podcasts. I'd hear somebody on one podcast and then listen to them on another. That's when I started listening to audiobooks, which allowed me to gain knowledge from books.

My sister, Abigail, actually introduced me to two people who changed my life: Ed Mylett and Andy Frisella. Ed Mylett really resonated with me with the way he interviewed people and shared their stories. I began hearing about successful people and how success leaves clues. I started noticing commonalities among the people he interviewed. His interviewing style focused on where people came from, their backgrounds, how they became successful, what they're doing now, and how they plan to stay successful. So, I started listening to them more and more and taking action. I sought information from every possible source. Through Ed Mylett, I discovered Brendan Burchard. One of the first books I read that stood out to me was *High Performance Habits: How Extraordinary People Become That Way,* written by Brendon Burchard. This book delved into the underlying habits that enable individuals to perform at an elite level in various aspects of life, including career, personal development, and relationships.

Burchard's work is based on extensive research, including one of the largest studies of high performers ever conducted. He identifies six core habits that are essential for achieving high performance:

1. *Seeking Clarity*: Understanding one's goals and aligning them with daily actions.

2. *Generating Energy*: Actively cultivating mental, emotional, and physical energy.

3. *Raising Necessity*: Creating a sense of urgency and personal accountability for performance.

4. *Increasing Productivity*: Focusing on what truly matters and avoiding unnecessary distractions.

5. *Developing Influence*: Building strong relationships and leading others effectively.

6. *Demonstrating Courage*: Taking bold actions and standing firm in the face of challenges.

These habits are not exclusive to any particular field or profession; they can be applied by anyone seeking to improve their performance and reach their highest potential.

The book is divided into sections that explain each habit in detail and provide practical tools and exercises to help integrate the principles into daily life. I highly recommend it to anyone interested in personal growth, leadership, and achieving success in any domain.

I just kept going down the rabbit hole with habits, so I read more books. Next was *The Power of Habit: Why We Do What We Do in Life and Business,* written by Charles Duhigg. It was published in 2012 and explores the science behind why habits are formed, how they function, and how they can be changed.

- *The Habit Loop*: Duhigg introduces the idea of the "habit loop," which consists of three components: the cue, the routine, and the reward. The cue triggers the routine (or habit), and the reward reinforces the habit loop.

- *Keystone Habits*: The book emphasizes that some habits, known as "keystone habits," have the power to initiate a chain reaction, changing other habits and many aspects of one's life.

- *Habit Formation in Organizations*: Duhigg also applies the principles of habit formation to businesses and organizations, illustrating how habits can be leveraged to improve organizational performance.

- *Changing Habits*: The book provides insight into how habits can be altered by understanding the underlying cue and reward and then consciously developing a new routine to respond to the cue.

- *Social Habits*: Duhigg delves into the habits of societies and how they influence social norms and movements. He explores how understanding and manipulating habits can lead to profound societal changes.

- *Case Studies*: Throughout the book, various case studies and real-life examples are used to illustrate the principles of habit formation and change. These include personal stories, corporate examples, and societal observations.

The Power of Habit offers a comprehensive exploration of how habits work at the individual, organizational, and societal levels. It provides practical insights into understanding, managing, and changing habits, making it a valuable resource for personal development and organizational improvement.

The 3rd book on my Habit Hole journey was *Atomic Habits* by James Clear.

Atomic Habits is a book focused on the power of habits and how small, incremental changes can lead to significant improvement in one's life. James Clear, the author, emphasizes the importance of focusing on systems rather than goals, and he presents a comprehensive guide on forming good habits and breaking bad ones.

- *The Compound Effect of Habits*: The book stresses that even tiny changes, if consistent, can lead to significant improvements over time. These atomic (small) habits compound, producing enormous results in the long run.

- *The Four Laws of Behavior Change*: Clear introduces a framework to create good habits and eliminate bad ones:

    a. **Make It Obvious:** Increase awareness of the cues that trigger habits, making it easier to establish new ones.

    b. **Make It Attractive:** Associate positive feelings with the habit to make it more appealing.

    c. **Make It Easy:** Reduce friction and make the habit as simple as possible to perform.

    d. **Make It Satisfying:** Provide immediate satisfaction or rewards, reinforcing the habit.

- *Identity-Based Habits*: Clear emphasizes that habits are connected to one's identity. Changing habits involves changing the perception of oneself. By believing in a new identity, one can create habits that align with that identity.

- *Habit Stacking*: This technique involves linking a new habit to an existing one. By attaching a new habit to a specific cue or existing routine, it becomes easier to remember and implement.

- *Environment Design*: Clear advises on designing the environment to support the desired habits. Removing temptations and making good habits more accessible can be powerful tools in habit formation.

- *Tracking and Accountability*: The book suggests using habit tracking to make progress visible and maintain motivation. Accountability partners or systems can also help in staying committed.

- *Understanding the Habit Loop*: Clear explains the cue-craving-response-reward loop that governs habit formation. Understanding this loop enables more effective control over habits.

- *Utilizing the Two-Minute Rule*: If a new habit takes less than two minutes to do, it can be a gateway to a larger routine. Starting small makes new habits more manageable.

Atomic Habits presents a practical and systematic approach to habit formation, emphasizing the profound impact of small, consistent changes. By focusing on process and identity and utilizing specific techniques and principles, individuals can transform their lives through the power of habits.

I started implementing a lot of habits into my life. I also learned about habit stacking and how to use it as a strategy for building new habits by linking them to existing routines or behaviors that are already established in your daily life. By connecting a new habit to something you already do regularly, you can create a natural cue for the new behavior, making it easier to remember and integrate into your routine.

Here's a simple explanation of habit stacking:

1. *Identify an Existing Habit*: Choose a habit or routine that you already perform consistently, like brushing your teeth in the morning.

2. *Choose a New Habit*: Decide on a new habit you want to develop, such as taking vitamins.

3. *Link the New Habit to the Existing One*: Combine the new habit with the existing one by performing them consecutively. For example, every time you brush your teeth, you'll then take your vitamins.

4. *Repeat Consistently*: By repeatedly performing the new habit right after the existing one, it becomes a natural part of your routine.

The advantage of habit stacking is that it leverages the power of existing habits to create a strong trigger for the new behavior. This can make it easier to establish new habits without relying on willpower alone. It's a practical approach to building positive routines that can be applied to various aspects of personal growth and development.

For me, it was making my bed first thing when I woke up, then brushing my teeth. I incorporated stretching and breathing exercises into that routine every morning to help me start my day. From having these habits set, everything else flowed. These habits kept me consistent even when motivation was lacking. Brendan Burchard has a great analogy that compares the human body and mind to a power plant. Unlike a traditional power plant that simply consumes energy from an external source, he argues that humans have the ability to generate their own energy. This energy isn't just physical; it encompasses mental and emotional energy as well.

- *Generating Energy*: A power plant doesn't have energy; it generates energy. Similarly, individuals can actively create mental, emotional, and physical energy rather than waiting for it to come from external sources.

- Mental Energy: This refers to the ability to maintain focus, clarity, and a positive mindset. By actively managing thoughts and beliefs, individuals can generate the mental energy required to pursue goals and stay engaged.

- *Emotional Energy*: Emotional energy is about cultivating positive emotions like joy, gratitude, and confidence. Burchard encourages practices like meditation, reflection, and connection with others to build a reservoir of positive emotional energy.

- *Physical Energy*: This includes taking care of the body through proper nutrition, exercise, and sleep. Like maintaining the machinery in a power plant, taking care of one's physical health ensures that the "human power plant" runs efficiently.

- *Maintenance and Renewal*: Just as a power plant requires regular maintenance and renewal of its parts, individuals must consistently invest in practices that renew and sustain their energy levels. This includes both daily habits and periodic breaks to rejuvenate.

The power plant analogy talks about the idea that energy isn't something that merely happens to us; it's something we can actively cultivate. Adopting specific strategies and practices can generate the energy needed to perform at high levels in every aspect of life.

I love the power plant analogy because it paints a vivid picture of "Generating Energy" and your proactive role in cultivating mental, emotional, and physical energy to drive success and personal growth. For me, it's non-negotiable.

I always woke up early to go to work in manufacturing. I would start my day by making my bed, and then slowly, I started stacking on new habits. I knew reading was one of the main ways that I could learn more and that most successful people read books. So, I started looking at what most successful people do. I began studying millionaire morning routines, started listening to what Ed Mylett did for his morning routine, and started listening to what Andy Frisella did for his lifestyle. I just started getting curious. I began listening and implementing. I was at a point where my life was nothing like I wanted it to be. I wanted to change. I was always a skeptical person, probably because of the way I was raised and because of how my dad was. I was skeptical about doing certain things, but I decided no matter how cheesy or cliché certain things sounded to me, I would do them and see if they worked for me.

My desire to change outweighed my excuses at that point, and I just started trying everything I heard successful people were doing. I began seeing what worked for me and what didn't, and I started implementing and adjusting. I started reading two pages of a book a day. I thought, *If I can just do that every day, I'll at least get better at it.* I would make my bed, get up, and read two pages of a book. I would write different things. I learned about affirmations, which I prefer to call declarations because I like to declare who I want to be. What are the actions? What are the things that the person you want to be does? What are the attributes and the characteristics? What are the actions that the person you want to become takes on a day-to-day basis? How do they think? So that's the way I look at my affirmations and declarations now. I started learning about all of these things and slowly implementing them into my life. It wasn't an easy, quick change overnight. I didn't just find out about these things and then overnight, my life was fixed. I was still dealing with the environment that I was in.

I think mindset is one of the biggest factors you have to change when it comes to your weight. That's what I discovered in my weight loss journey. I would always yo-yo up and down in weight, and it was because I had a goal, and I would just try to reach it. Once I achieved it, I would go back to my old habits. So, I decided to start living an active, healthy lifestyle instead of just aiming for a goal weight. I took a year off from going to the gym and began doing activities like rock climbing, kayaking, jogging, hiking, and cycling. I told myself I would do everything possible to maintain an active lifestyle, eat healthier, and change my mindset about exercise and weight. I wanted to establish healthy habits for my future self, and that's how I managed to break the yo-yo pattern in my weight loss journey. Changing my mindset and focusing on long-term fitness rather than short-term goals was key. I aimed to be active well into my 60s, 70s, 80s, and 90s rather than trying to achieve the bodybuilder or GQ model figure that society often deems as the ideal.

There were times when I thought I wanted to become a bodybuilder, so I'd hit the gym and lift weights with my ego. Unfortunately, I ended up injuring myself multiple times. I realized I needed to be more consistent and form healthier habits. I decided to focus on consistency and establishing habits for my future self rather than just losing weight and reverting to my old ways.

I was still on probation from my first DWI, and I had quit drinking to lose weight. Since I was on probation, I wanted to complete it without any incidents related to alcohol. I managed to go ten months without drinking, but I hadn't changed my environment or the people I was around. Eventually, I found myself in a situation where I was with people who were using drugs. After dealing with a chaotic week of being around individuals on drugs, I reached a breaking point and decided to go get drunk. After ten months of sobriety, I turned off my self-control and decided to party. I always had people to go out and party with, and as soon as I started drinking again, everyone was happy to see me join in. It was as if "misery loves company."

During my sober months, I didn't socialize as much, but when I started drinking again, everyone was eager to hang out with me. Cocaine was also readily available in those circles, even if I didn't procure it myself. I went on a two- or three-day bender with friends and felt terrible about it afterward. I returned to not drinking for a while in an attempt to get back on track. Preparing for setbacks is crucial when you don't have healthy coping mechanisms or established habits. I worked on finding my rhythm and identifying strategies to get back on track as quickly as possible.

Exercise played a crucial role. If I returned to exercising and eating healthily, I knew I would get back on track more easily. Additionally, the older I got, the longer it took me to recover from hangovers, which also had a mental toll. I tend to be hard on myself, and as I set more goals for myself, any deviation from those goals led to self-criticism. As I learned more about personal growth and development, I realized the importance of understanding the "why" behind your goals. Figuring out the reasons for what you're doing is crucial. Initially, I didn't know my "why." I simply knew I wanted to change. But as I got older and family became more important to me, it became easier to identify my "whys."

An excellent book that helps you understand the importance of your "why" is *Start with Why* by Simon Sinek. It delves into the idea that successful individuals and organizations are clear about their "why" — their purpose, cause, or belief that inspires them to do what they do. While most companies can articulate WHAT they do and HOW they do it, few can articulate WHY. Sinek argues that companies and leaders that operate from a clear sense of WHY are able to inspire others and achieve lasting success.

The Golden Circle: Sinek introduces a model called the Golden Circle, which comprises three layers:

1. WHY (the core belief of the business, why the business exists)
2. HOW (the values and principles that guide how the business works)
3. WHAT (the products or services the business offers).

Inspiration Over Manipulation: Companies that communicate from the inside out of the Golden Circle (starting with WHY) are more able to inspire and build trust with their customers, as opposed to those that rely on manipulations like price reductions or promotions.

The Law of Diffusion of Innovation: Sinek discusses this law, which explains how an idea or product gains traction and becomes widely adopted. He correlates this with the importance of targeting a company's most loyal customers, the "early adopters," who believe in the company's WHY and can drive its success.

Leadership and Trust: The book emphasizes that true leaders are those who lead with WHY, inspire others to follow, and create an environment built on trust.

The WHY Must Be Clear: Organizations that have a clear WHY have a consistent filter for making decisions that align with their core belief. Without a clear WHY, companies may drift from one strategy to another without a cohesive direction.

Sustainability and Adaptation: Organizations with a clear WHY are not just focused on short-term achievements; they are better positioned to adapt and thrive in the long term.

Apple as a Case Study: Apple is frequently cited in the book as a company that leads with its WHY, focusing on challenging the status quo and thinking differently. This has allowed Apple to inspire loyalty among its customers and succeed in various product categories.

The book *Start with Why* underscores the significance of understanding and articulating the deeper purpose behind what we do. It suggests that when actions and decisions stem from a clear WHY, they resonate more deeply and lead to lasting success and impact.

As I distanced myself from my old partying lifestyle and the people associated with it, I began to realize that the ones who remained unwaveringly supportive were my family. My mom had taken care of us, helped us obtain our birth certificates and social security numbers, and raised us. She provided me with a place to live when I left my dad's. I always assisted her with the bills, and we lived together several times over the years. My sisters were a constant source of support. I wanted to give back and share the kinds of experiences I had come to value, such as going out on boats and enjoying a different quality of life. My aim was to provide these experiences for my mom and sisters, set a positive example for my nieces and nephews, and discover more profound reasons for pursuing my goals.

My motivations evolved as I considered the future. I started thinking about my mom's retirement, her lack of savings due to her past relationship with my dad, and who would take care of her as she aged. None of my sisters and I were financially well-off. My mom lived alone in an apartment, and although we were geographically close, I desired closer bonds with her and my sisters after years of pursuing my own path, working, partying, and self-discovery. I yearned for more family time, to build stronger connections with them, and to support my mom in her retirement. Providing for her and covering her living expenses became one of my most significant motivations.

When I purchased my first house, my mom moved in with me. Thanks to my success in real estate, she was able to semi-retire. Seeing some of my goals materialize was encouraging. I took her on a vacation, just the two of us, to Playa del Carmen earlier this year. It was a rewarding experience to witness the positive impact of the changes I'd made in my life, including taking care of her, within a relatively short time frame. However, these accomplishments would not have been possible if I hadn't started making gradual changes.

One thing I learned is that consistency is a rarity. I realized that one of my strengths was my ability to maintain consistency. I had always worked since I was 10 years old, and working was my comfort zone. To establish the habit of exercise, I treated it like work. I would go to the gym right after finishing my workday, tricking my mind into believing that my workday wasn't over until I completed my workout. This work ethic spilled over into other aspects of my life. When it came to real estate investing, I approached it with the same mentality. I formed habits around activities such as listening to podcasts, watching YouTube videos, and reading, treating them as work.

Although I initially disregarded a friend's suggestion that I get my real estate license, I met a guy who was a REALTOR®. Our conversation sparked my interest, as real estate had been on my mind. I've since learned about the RAS (Reticular Activating System), a part of the brain that filters information and focuses on what's important. When you consistently concentrate on something, your RAS recognizes opportunities, resources, and information related to that focus. So, by concentrating on my goals and real estate, I trained my RAS to notice relevant elements that could help me achieve those goals. Ed Mylett discusses this concept in detail in his book *The Power of One More.*

Later, I ran into that same guy at the gym who was a REALTOR®. We had met briefly during a double date with a girl I was seeing. As real estate was on my radar, I struck up a conversation with him. This chance encounter led to valuable information about the home-buying process and connections in the real estate world. The more I learned about real estate investing, the more I considered getting my real estate license, especially since I was becoming increasingly dissatisfied with my manufacturing job.

My original plan was to stay in my manufacturing job and use the money I earned to invest in real estate. However, the job became progressively less enjoyable, and I yearned for something more fulfilling. A significant turning point was when my boss, who had worked at the company for over 20 years, unexpectedly gave his two weeks' notice. It caught me off guard because I had always assumed I would quit before he did. His departure left me feeling adrift, and I made a poor choice. I fell back into my old habit of going out drinking with friends, which resulted in a car accident, my third arrest, and a significant wake-up call.

To be completely honest, the experience was both terrifying and embarrassing. I remember getting out of jail the next morning and having to call my sister to pick me up. I was devastated by how much progress I had made and the setbacks I had caused. I knew I had chosen to go out drinking, fully aware of the potential consequences. I took full responsibility for my actions. Instead of regretting what happened, I saw it as a catalyst for further change and a reminder that I had to transform every aspect of my life. I couldn't expect different results by doing the same things and hanging out with the same people. Through this event, I realized I had to change my mindset toward my lifestyle, just as I had changed my mindset about exercise.

It was the "burn the boats" moment for me. I knew I had to get out of the career that I was in, get off the merry-go-round, and change my life completely. It was clear that I needed to do something different that was scary and out of my comfort zone. I had already started doing those things, but this arrest was the final straw. I had decided to get my real estate license and worked on it every day, two hours a day after work, while keeping up with all my other exercise habits and routines.

I got my real estate license at the end of 2020 and started apartment locating while still working full-time in manufacturing. I was working about 80 hours a week in order to save up enough money to quit my job in manufacturing to go full-time into commission-based selling in residential real estate. I was able to do that at the end of 2021. I quit apartment locating, quit my manufacturing job, and went into residential real estate full-time. That was the best decision I ever made. I can definitely say that real estate probably saved my life.

If I had stayed in that lifestyle and stayed around the same people that I had been around, then I don't know if I'd still be around. That last run-in with the law was definitely a time when I could have died or killed someone else. And I'm truly grateful that neither one of those things happened. It was a great catalyst to set me up for where I am now. I don't regret that life I lived because if I hadn't gone through it, I wouldn't know how much more there is in life.

Life has more to offer than the ordinary, normal life of mediocrity. I used to think that because of how I was raised, I couldn't accomplish anything more than a normal life. But I realized that because of how I was raised, I wasn't created to be normal. I was created to be extraordinary. And that's where I'm moving towards in my life continually. People think life and success are usually a straight shot, an easy path, but it's a roller coaster. A lot of times, you have setbacks, you have things that get in your way, it's an uphill battle, and there's definitely no easy way to success.

American novelist Tom Clancy famously said in his book *Dead or Alive*, "An overnight success is ten years in the making" because nobody sees the story behind the success. They don't know everything that it took to get there. So that's one of the reasons I'm writing this book, to show all of the trials and tribulations and the things that I went through that most people go through and that those things don't have to define your life. You can use those to catapult you to greatness, to catapult your life, and change your life. I've realized that it's a marathon. It's not a sprint. Or I like thinking of it as a marathon of sprints! Finish one sprint and then start another. It's something that you're always going to be working on. And there's no finish line. You're just going to keep going.

When you accomplish your childhood goal to have a normal life, and you find out that a normal life sucks... Well, you have to set a new goal.

You have to create a new dream to pursue, something else to work towards. Many scientific studies show that pursuing a goal is often more rewarding than actually getting to the goal. I highly recommend listening to Ed Mylett's podcast with Dr. Andrew Huberman titled "Unleash Your Brain Power and Growth Mindset." On that podcast, Dr. Huberman explains that "Dopamine is released anytime we experience something we really like, but under very specific conditions. Anytime we are moving towards something, and when we think we're on the right path, dopamine is released. And this is nature's way of telling whatever neurons are active during that movement down that path. So this could be exercise. It could be a relationship breakthrough. ... It could be learning some little piece of a puzzle that you're excited to learn."

Contrary to popular belief, dopamine is not released when you get a reward but released when you recognize that you're on the right path to getting a reward.

Dopamine shapes your brain so that when released, you naturally want to continue down that path. Dr. Huberman Continues, "Dopamine naturally causes neuroplasticity of whatever brain circuits were active previously. So it says, 'Hey, whatever I did to get to this point, this milestone, not the finish line, that is something that I might want to repeat reflexively in the future.'"

This is such an awesome thing to understand because the pleasure you get from dopamine is obtained not by accomplishing your goals but by striving toward them. It doesn't matter if you don't fully accomplish what you were striving towards — you're STILL going to get that pleasure from dopamine if you just try. It doesn't matter if you finish first or last in a sporting event or if you do or don't get that promotion you were competing for. As long as you are working toward your goal, your body will release dopamine, a chemical often associated with your overall well-being and happiness. You don't have to get everything that you want in life to be happy — you just need to PURSUE growth.

Ed Mylett also has a concept that really hits home for me, "Blissful Dissatisfaction."

"Blissful Dissatisfaction" is the balance between appreciating and enjoying one's current state, achievements, and possessions (the "blissful" part) while simultaneously having a desire for more or an ambition to achieve greater things (the "dissatisfaction" part).

Purpose: The idea is to prevent complacency and stagnation in one's life. While it's crucial to be grateful for what one has, it's equally important not to become too comfortable and lose the drive to pursue bigger goals or dreams.

Application in Daily Life: This concept encourages individuals to:

- Celebrate and acknowledge their current achievements.
- Maintain a clear vision of their next goals, keeping the ambition alive.
- Not allow contentment to deter them from striving for more.

Benefits:

- Provides a sustainable way to pursue personal growth without burning out.
- Encourages gratitude for the present moment while fostering ambition.
- Helps in maintaining motivation over the long term by balancing satisfaction with the drive to achieve more.

In essence, "Blissful Dissatisfaction" is about finding happiness in the present moment while keeping an eye on the future and continuing to pursue one's ambitions.

Accomplishing my only goal as a child — to have a normal life — was very anticlimactic!

After going through all of the trials and hardships that I went through and then discovering personal growth and all of the tools, tactics, and habits that lead to success, there's no going back. It's one of those things where you can't unsee it once you see it.

I think the tests that we go through in life can sometimes be the testimonies that will help others find their purpose. And that's what I want to do for you as the reader.

CHAPTER 3

THE EXTRAORDINARY LIFE

One of my favorite sayings is, "When the pain of the current reality becomes greater than the fear of change, that's when we change." My desire to change outweighed any of the excuses I had, especially after being arrested three times. There was really no turning back. Moving forward is all I could see. I believe everything happens for a reason. "Life Happens For You, Not to You." What happened *for* me really turned out to be a good thing.

After ten years, ten months, and 24 days at Thermon, I quit and went full-time into real estate to be my own boss. It was a major turning point in my story, completely giving something up that I had done for so long. It was like letting a part of me die. It often requires sacrifice and the death of who you once were to get to who you want to be. There's a price to be paid.

I had already started listening to a lot of successful people and business owners. So, I knew that I needed to treat my real estate business as a business owner from the start and not like a part-time employee!

I started learning as much as I could. Education was something that had never really been offered in manufacturing; it wasn't provided, and there was no required continuing education.

The required CE in real estate was one of the things that I liked about becoming a REALTOR®; the fact that there was always continuing education that you had to be taking and always opportunities for improvement. Not having a cap on my potential or my pay, knowing that however much work I put into it was what I was going to get out of it, I really took that to heart.

I was fortunate to have my mentor, Colum. I was going to go work with him at Keller Williams, but about a month before I quit my job at Thermon, he had moved brokerages to eXp Realty, and he showed me the eXp model in a 9-minute video, and I was hooked. I immediately understood the massive opportunity. I saw the financial opportunity. I got into real estate because of real estate investing to generate passive income. And with eXp Realty, the model has passive income in the form of revenue share. It also has stock options and stock rewards for your work achievements, by getting ownership in the company that I worked for and still getting to run my business the way that I wanted to. It was a no-brainer. It's nothing like any of the traditional models of real estate. I looked into and interviewed with a few other brokerages, J.B. Goodwin, Keller Williams, and Century 21, and they just can't compete with eXp when it comes to my long-term goals. And one of the aspects of this company is it's also cloud-based. So, I get to work from home.

I wanted to be able to get the most out of my time. I saw this brokerage as an opportunity to be free from commuting to someplace where bosses looked over my shoulder, or people told me what I needed to do. I'm very self-motivated. I wanted to do it on my own.

Colum challenged me on many things; he always wanted me to get out of my comfort zone. Going from working in a warehouse with the same five guys for almost 11 years to now being in a profession where I'm a salesperson, and my whole job is going out and meeting people, making relationships, networking, and putting myself out there on social media was terrifying. They don't tell you when you're getting into the real estate business that you will have to do all those things.

A lot of times, I think REALTORS® just think, *Oh, I get in, and I help people buy and sell homes, and that's going to be easy!* There's so much more that goes into it than that if you want to be successful in this business, treating it like a business and learning every aspect of running a business, from taxes to marketing, branding, video content, the list goes on and on.

There's always something to do. And that's part of what I love about it. I'm always able to learn, and there are classes provided to me at a relatively low cost. That was one of the things about real estate that appealed to me: I paid for the education and then went immediately into the field to start making money instead of going to college, where I have to take all of these courses to get a degree that I'm probably not going to use. It just made sense to me.

My mentor (the guy I met on a double date who I then ran into at the gym), Colum, challenged me to go out and start networking because I was just taking classes at first and getting set up and probably not taking enough action as I should have been. I looked up events in my area and went to my first networking meeting; I didn't even know what networking was at that time. Colum had told me about the local Chamber of Commerce and said I should sign up for that. I found another group called the Texas Emerging Leaders, a networking organization in my area, and I just decided to go.

I didn't know anybody when I showed up at the end of December 2021. I was super introverted, shy, and self-conscious, unaware of my body language, and lacked talking points. But I just started saying hi to people;

I didn't really know what I was doing. Fortunately, I met a guy named Mike, who was very outgoing. He started introducing me to people. Towards the end of the event, he introduced me to a mortgage lender, and I really wanted to learn more about the mortgage process.

It takes 180 hours to become a REALTOR® in the state of Texas, and it's a broad overview. Texas is one of the states that has the highest standard of education to become a REALTOR®. Some states have 40 to 60 hours, up to 135, but Texas tops them all, requiring 180 hours. And it still doesn't really cover anything to do with mortgages. I just started talking to him and learning from him. When the event was over, we exchanged information and got together outside the event. He worked out of his house, which was cool. Getting to meet more people who worked from home was something that was never an option for me in the manufacturing industry.

He was very intelligent, passionate, and analytical with his numbers. He explained how the mortgage process worked and how to help renters become buyers. I just learned as much as possible from him and met with him one or two more times, soaking up all the knowledge he was willing to give me. Out of that, he gave me my first buyer client. He sent me a message saying, *"Hey, I've got a first-time pre-qualified home buyer. I'm sending him your information and one other REALTOR®'s information."*

I was able to get on the phone with the guy and set up showings. I had started networking more. I went to a "Lunch and Learn" event with an organization called the New Braunfels Jaycees, the Junior Chamber of Commerce, here in my city. They had the city commissioner do a presentation about all the growth statistics of our city. It was really informative. I was able to immediately drive my buyer around and show him seven houses, telling him about the community and all the growth statistics and demographics—everything I had just learned from that meeting. We ended up finding a house that he liked and put in an offer. That was my first buyer sale.

What I learned from experiences like that one was that by doing things that were out of my comfort zone, I got positive results. It was encouraging to see that I put myself out there, got uncomfortable, had conversations, met people, got curious, was open to learning, and had genuine curiosity and the intention to be able to repeat and teach what I had just learned. It helped give my buyer confidence in me, to use me as his REALTOR® and allow me to help him purchase his first home.

That was eye-opening to me. When all of that happened, it was like, "Okay, I need to do these things that take me out of my comfort zone, and I'll get results." So, I continually put myself out there, went to networking events, started recording some videos, learned how social media worked, and took classes about anything that would help me grow.

In my first two weeks as a residential REALTOR®, I also got my first listing, and that was from going to the gym and doing something out of my comfort zone. Fitness is a major part of my life, so going to the gym was normal. I've had some workout partners in the past, but I usually go work out by myself. I didn't like being in classes thinking other people were watching me or that I couldn't keep up with the other people in the class, but I decided to go to a group cycling class at my gym and get out of my comfort zone. Well, it paid off. I overheard the cycling instructor talking to another class member, saying she was moving to California, so I struck up a conversation with her.

"Oh, I heard you were moving."

And she said, "Yeah, I am."

I said, "Well, I'm a REALTOR®."

"Do you want to sell my house?" she asked.

"Yes," I replied enthusiastically.

So that was my first listing appointment within two weeks of becoming a REALTOR®. I didn't know what I was doing at my first listing presentation. I went to my mentor Colum and asked him what to do, and he gave me some great advice. I created a listing presentation and printed it out for when I went and looked at their home. I did my best with what I knew at that time, and I got the listing. I was able to list the property and get it sold for them within a short time.

I realized that doing uncomfortable things and being consistent with them was crucial to staying on track. In February 2022, I decided to start a program called "75 HARD," created by Andy Frisella, the founder of 1st Phorm Nutrition. It's a challenging program designed to foster mental toughness and physical discipline. I had wanted to do it while working in manufacturing, but I couldn't justify waking up any earlier than my usual 2:45 a.m. start time, given that I was already waking up so early.

Participants in the 75 HARD program must commit to the following daily tasks:

1. Follow a structured diet plan aimed at physical improvement (no deviations allowed).
2. Abstain from alcohol.
3. Complete two 45-minute workouts, one of which must be outdoors.
4. Take a progress photo.
5. Consume one gallon of water.
6. Read ten pages of a non-fiction book (audiobooks not included).

Moreover, no modifications to the program are permitted, and if you fail to meet any of these daily goals, you must restart from day one.

I reached a point where I had run out of excuses not to do it. It was necessary because I felt like I was just going through the motions — working out regularly and reading often, but not making reading a daily habit. I had started slacking off and sleeping in later. Throughout my manufacturing career, I had always been an early riser, and sleeping in until seven or eight in the morning didn't align with the type of person I wanted to become.

I knew that being a business owner would require me to rise early and accomplish things for myself before tending to others' needs. Establishing this routine seemed far more productive than rolling out of bed and immediately reacting to the day's events. So, on Thursday, February 24, 2022, I made the decision to start 75 HARD.

I chose to eliminate all desserts, as I have a sweet tooth, and that's one of my weaknesses. Additionally, I cut out red meat and primarily focused on a diet consisting of chicken, fish, veggies, nuts, and grains. I reduced my pasta and carb intake. The key aspects of my diet that I committed to were avoiding desserts and candies. I also made sure to read ten pages of a book daily, completed my workouts, and listened to books and podcasts during my jogs.

During this time, I started listening to the book *Iron Cowboy*, which tells the remarkable story of James Lawrence, a renowned triathlete and motivational speaker. He earned the nickname "Iron Cowboy" for his incredible feat of completing 50 Ironman triathlons in 50 consecutive days, covering all 50 U.S. states.

An Ironman triathlon consists of a grueling 2.4-mile swim, a challenging 112-mile bicycle ride, and an exhausting 26.2-mile marathon run.

Lawrence's journey wasn't just a physical challenge but also a mental one. The book delved into the psychological aspects of his achievement, exploring his motivation, determination, and strategies to conquer the immense physical and mental hurdles to achieve his goal.

His story served as an inspiring testament to human endurance and potential, offering insights into the power of persistence, resilience, and unwavering self-belief. It provided a detailed account of what it takes to push the boundaries of human capabilities and achieve what many would deem impossible.

As I embarked on the 75 HARD Program, I thought a lot about how much more challenging it could be. Hearing about the incredible capabilities of the human body and the need to reprogram one's mindset to conquer pain was truly mind-blowing. During the initial weeks, I diligently completed all the daily tasks, drawing motivation from sources like David Goggins and other inspirational figures.

After a while, the program became less challenging, and I just kept going with it. As the 75 days neared completion, I found myself accomplishing all the tasks each day, transforming the way I approached everything. I became much more productive, eliminating excuses. I also managed to shed some weight, going from 205 pounds down to 185 pounds in those 75 days. But I wasn't done; I decided to continue. The essence of 75 HARD is to reshape oneself, forging a stronger and better version of "you." It builds grit and mental toughness, and it certainly did that for me. I thought, *Why not go for another 75 days?* So, I made it to 150 days, and then I kept going. I reached 180 days of completing all the daily tasks.

My business started thriving, and the program helped me maintain a disciplined work ethic. I firmly believe that keeping the promises we make to ourselves each day and demonstrating personal integrity by doing what we say we'll do boosts confidence. My confidence increased, my personal health and well-being improved, and I stayed healthy — never contracting COVID, which I attribute to the exercise and lifestyle fostered by 75 HARD.

After 180 days, I stopped doing some of the tasks but maintained the habit of working out twice a day and reading daily. Currently, I'm on day 560 of working out twice daily and reading at least 10 pages of personal growth, development, or business literature every day. I may have missed reading for three or four days, but I had an excuse: I was attending a Tony Robbins event, Unleash the Power Within, in November 2022. I remained committed to my workouts, considering them non-negotiable. This routine significantly contributes to my mental clarity and physical well-being. Getting outside, soaking in the sun, and gaining energy from that while listening to podcasts and audiobooks has become a daily necessity for me.

When the topic comes up in conversation, I share what I do with people, and one person likened it to "downloading information like they did in *The Matrix*." I hadn't thought about it in those terms, but essentially, yes, I've been so consistent in listening to and reading materials every day to enhance my life and accelerate my personal growth. In a way, it's like downloading information, just like *The Matrix* movie.

Through networking, meeting other professionals, and learning about running a business, I crossed paths with a coach at one of these events, Dr. Caitlin Walker. Her energetic and professional demeanor during her elevator pitch stood out to me. Her profession, coaching, was something I had never encountered in real life. While I had heard successful people mention coaching on podcasts, like Ed Mylett's, I had always associated it with wealthy individuals and hadn't considered it for myself. However, with my commitment to change my life, I decided to give it a shot.

I scheduled a consultation with Dr. Walker and had a positive gut feeling about her. After hiring her and embarking on our coaching journey, she pointed out that during our initial encounter at the networking event, I appeared closed off. My body language, demeanor, tone of voice, and even my smile were indicators of my discomfort and fear in social settings. Working with her, we delved into body language, self-awareness, and effective communication. She helped me understand and improve how I presented myself, from smiling more in pictures to uncrossing my arms and adopting an open posture. I learned about colors and branding, and her guidance made me a more adept business owner. Over several months of working with her, my eyes were opened to a new world of self-awareness and personal growth I had never before experienced.

"You don't know what you don't know."

After experiencing the immense value she brought to my life and witnessing how she helped me break out of my shell, I decided I wanted to do the same for others. I began researching coaching and the available coaching certifications. I live in a town with Texas State University, which offers a continuing education program. After thorough research, I discovered a Certified Professional Life Coach Certification course there. While it was the most expensive class I had ever enrolled in (real estate education was comparably less costly), I decided to take the leap. The course cost $1,800 and involved 40 hours of training. Although it was a financial stretch for me, my passion for acquiring these skills and helping others compelled me to pursue it.

This coaching certification led me through a series of exercises and training tools, teaching me the techniques I would later use with my clients. I set goals, clarified my values, defined my mission, and identified my WHY. Understanding my reasons for wanting to change my life and move forward was pivotal to my personal journey. The coaching course also helped me recognize and confront disempowering beliefs and self-limiting thoughts that hinder personal growth. It delved deeply into habits and environment, revealing that everything I had done on my own prior to the course aligned with the coaching techniques I was learning.

This realization was affirming and validating, as it demonstrated that the results I had achieved had been accomplished using these techniques, even before I knew about them. I understood that much of my success came from modeling the behaviors of successful individuals, as success leaves clues. I recognized that many people had already navigated the challenges I was facing and possessed knowledge that could expedite my own journey.

Following this certification, I had another opportunity come up. My brokerage, eXp Realty, had acquired *SUCCESS* Magazine, a publication with a history dating back to 1897. From this acquisition, they established SUCCESS Coaching, led by Jairek Robbins, who happened to be Tony Robbins' son. I decided to pursue certification with SUCCESS Coaching despite the cost being an even greater stretch at $5,000. I understood that this investment would help me achieve my goals and enable me to assist more people worldwide.

The 40-hour coaching course was an incredible experience. I trained with outstanding coaches who shared my growth-oriented mindset.

Meeting people who were passionate about helping others and self-improvement was refreshing. However, it was also overwhelming, as there was so much to learn. I felt like I was in a state of conscious incompetence, recognizing that there was still much more to grasp.

Through SUCCESS Coaching, I had the privilege of meeting Brian Mayoral, one of Tony Robbins' top Peak Performance strategists, who had broken 40-year sales records during the time he worked with Tony. Brian had started his own company called SellUp, and Brian's approach to sales was unique, as it stemmed from a coaching perspective rather than traditional high-pressure sales tactics. I learned that Brian taught others how to sell effectively through his company, SellUp. I enrolled in his 8-week SellUp Sales Mastery Certification class, even though it came at a hefty price tag of $6,500. Troy Wahl, who was one of Brian's best salesmen, helped me to believe in myself and that this investment would not only improve my real estate sales skills but also enhance my communication abilities for coaching.

Upon completing the course, I got the opportunity to work part-time for Brian, and I seized it. I understood that immersing myself in sales would sharpen my skills, and I firmly believed that proximity is power. Learning from Brian Mayoral and being mentored by him provided invaluable insights and access to other high-performing individuals. I forged connections with remarkable people during the course and while working with Brian. One individual who stood out was Patricija from Slovenia. Her vibrant energy and inspirational personality motivated me to take more action and become more outgoing.

Brian's entire team was incredible, supporting and encouraging my growth. During my part-time work for Brian, I also had the chance to help sell courses for Dr. Delatorro L. McNeal, Dr. Alok Trivedi, and Todd

Hartley. This exposure allowed me to gain a deeper understanding of their businesses and adapt their strategies to my own.

I firmly believe that everything happens for a reason, and the chain of events that led to writing this book would not have occurred if I had not ventured into coaching and working for SUCCESS Coaching.

As part of my real estate business, I utilize social media, and one day, I posted an Instagram reel discussing my transition from manufacturing to real estate. Cris Cawley, the founder of Game Changer Publishing, came across my post and reached out to me personally. I researched her and Game Changer Publishing and discovered that they had published books for Dr. Delatorro L. McNeal and Dr. Alok Trivedi, which solidified her credibility.

This book project wouldn't have been possible without the serendipitous chain of events that brought Cris Cawley into my life. I believe it was a result of the Law of Attraction, my willingness to step out of my comfort zone, and my perception of every situation as an opportunity or an "open door." Recognizing when to walk through those open doors and seize the opportunity can be the difference between living an ordinary life and an extraordinary one.

One of my favorite sayings about luck is, "Luck is when preparation meets opportunity."

The Law of Attraction really opened my mind. *The Secret*, written by Rhonda Byrne, is a book based on the Law of Attraction, which emphasizes how thoughts can influence a person's reality.

The Secret introduces the concept that the universe operates according to the Law of Attraction. According to this law, positive or negative thoughts bring corresponding positive or negative experiences into a person's life. The book provides practical guidance and techniques on how to apply this law, suggesting that by focusing on positive thoughts and feelings, individuals can attract success, wealth, happiness, and health.

- *Law of Attraction*: The central tenet of the book states that like attracts like. Positive thoughts attract positive outcomes, while negative thoughts bring about negative results.

- *Visualization*: It encourages readers to visualize their desires as if they have already been fulfilled, thereby attracting them into reality.

- *Gratitude*: it emphasizes the importance of expressing gratitude for what one has, as it creates positive vibrations that attract more of what is desired.

- *Positive Affirmations*: It talks about the use of positive statements to overcome negative thoughts or self-limiting beliefs and aligning oneself with the desired outcomes.

- *Ask, Believe, Receive*: A three-step process outlining how to apply the Law of Attraction. It involves asking for what you want, believing that you will receive it, and then being open to receiving it.

I also learned about Positive Psychology during my coaching certification. This is a branch of psychology that focuses on the positive aspects of the human experience, such as happiness, well-being, and personal strengths. Dr. Martin Seligman, often referred to as the "father" of positive psychology, has been instrumental in shaping and promoting this field.

Positive psychology is an area of psychological study that emphasizes the positive qualities of human life rather than focusing solely on mental illness or deficits. It seeks to promote well-being, happiness, and fulfillment by understanding and cultivating positive emotions, strengths, and virtues.

1. **PERMA Model:** Seligman developed the PERMA model, which identifies five essential elements of well-being:

   - P: Positive Emotion
   - E: Engagement
   - R: Relationships
   - M: Meaning
   - A: Accomplishment

2. **Character Strengths and Virtues**: This concept emphasizes the identification and cultivation of individual strengths and virtues. The goal is to enable people to live a more authentic and fulfilling life by leveraging their unique positive traits.

3. **Learned Optimism**: Seligman's theory of learned optimism explores how individuals can develop a more optimistic outlook. This involves recognizing and challenging negative thoughts and fostering a sense of hope and resilience.

4. **Positive Interventions**: Seligman has advocated for the use of positive interventions, techniques, and practices that can enhance well-being and reduce depression. These can include gratitude exercises, mindfulness practices, and strengths-based approaches.

5. **Positive Education**: Seligman has also worked on integrating positive psychology principles into educational settings. This

approach emphasizes the development of character strengths, emotional intelligence, and well-being alongside traditional academic learning.

For those who may not know how to maintain a positive mindset or who find it challenging, there's an alternative called "Neutral Thinking," which can help counteract the pitfalls of "Toxic Positivity" in today's culture.

"Neutral Thinking" is a concept introduced by Trevor Moawad in his book, *It Takes What It Takes*. Unlike positive or negative thinking, neutral thinking emphasizes the importance of factual and objective understanding. Here are the key concepts of Neutral Thinking:

1. *Reality-Based Approach*: Instead of focusing on positive or negative outcomes, neutral thinking stresses the importance of understanding the current reality. It's about assessing situations based on facts, not emotions or biases.

2. *Avoiding Negativity*: Moawad posits that negative thoughts have a greater impact on our behavior and outcomes than positive thoughts. Neutral thinking, therefore, emphasizes reducing or eliminating negative self-talk rather than necessarily replacing it with positive affirmations.

3. *The Power of Language*: Words and internal dialogue play a significant role in shaping our actions. By being more deliberate about our language and avoiding extreme, negative words, we can influence our behavior in a more productive direction.

4. *Behavior Over Feelings*: Neutral thinking stresses the importance of focusing on one's actions and behaviors over feelings. Instead

of getting overwhelmed by the larger goal or outcome, it's about breaking things down into manageable actions.

5. *Process-Oriented Mindset*: This approach encourages individuals to concentrate on the processes and steps necessary to achieve an outcome rather than just the outcome itself. By staying neutral and focusing on the next action, individuals can navigate challenges more effectively.

6. *Response to Adversity*: Everyone faces challenges. Neutral thinking provides a framework to respond to adversity by assessing the situation without emotional biases and deciding on the most effective next step.

One of my favorite books is *Becoming Supernatural: How Common People Are Doing the Uncommon,* written by Dr. Joe Dispenza. It blends scientific research with practical guidance and empowers you to transcend their current limitations and beliefs.

- *Mind-Body Connection*: The book emphasizes the profound connection between the mind and the body. Dr. Dispenza argues that changing one's thoughts and emotions can have physiological effects.

- *Meditation and Visualization*: Through meditation and visualization techniques, the book guides readers on how to tap into their subconscious mind to promote healing and achieve desired outcomes.

- *Neuroplasticity*: The brain's ability to rewire itself. Dr. Dispenza explains how repetitive mental and emotional practice can create new neural pathways, leading to lasting changes in thoughts, behaviors, and life experiences.

- *Quantum Physics and Spirituality*: The book explores the intersection of quantum physics and spirituality. It presents the idea that thoughts and consciousness are energetic and can influence physical reality.

- *Heart Coherence*: Dr. Dispenza discusses the role of the heart in creating coherence within the body. By aligning thoughts and emotions, he believes that individuals can create a more harmonious state of being.

- *Practical Applications*: The book provides practical exercises and techniques, including guided meditations, to help readers apply the principles in their daily lives. The goal is to guide individuals in transcending their ordinary selves to unlock greater potential.

- *Scientific Approach*: Throughout the book, Dr. Dispenza supports his claims with scientific research, case studies, and personal anecdotes. This approach helps bridge the gap between spiritual practices and modern science.

After finishing the coaching certification, I was still doing real estate full-time and coaching as my passion, just learning more and more.

Jim Rohn has a quote, "Your level of success will seldom exceed your level of personal development because success is something you attract by the person you become."

I started realizing that the more I focused on improving myself, the more it would transfer over to my business and all aspects of my life. So, I just really dove deep into as much personal growth and development as I could; I was continually learning and challenging myself.

I attribute a lot of that to my success in doing the hard things at the beginning of the day that nobody wants to do. I've accomplished more than most people do all day before most people even wake up.

I think habits are the number one thing that I can attribute to my current level of success!

Standards Define Success: The standards you set for yourself determine the quality of your life. Your personal, professional, and financial success is a reflection of the standards you maintain.

Once I established these habits, education became more manageable, and I actively implemented what I learned. There's a saying from Brian Buffini that resonates with me: "Education without Implementation is Merely Entertainment." I took that saying to heart when I first heard it. I understood the importance of taking action, so I started applying what I learned, becoming more self-aware. I also have a penchant for taking tests, and I've undergone assessments such as the Gallup Clifton Strengths assessment, the DISC personality assessment, and several others.

The Gallup Clifton Strengths personality test, also known as CliftonStrengths, is a psychological assessment tool that focuses on identifying an individual's unique combination of talents and strengths. Grounded in positive psychology, its purpose is to enhance personal and professional development by helping individuals understand and leverage their innate abilities.

- *34 Themes of Talent*: The assessment identifies the presence of 34 distinct talent themes, categorized into four domains: Executing, Influencing, Relationship Building, and Strategic Thinking. These themes represent natural patterns of thinking, feeling, and behaving.

- *Top 5 Strengths*: Upon completion of the assessment, individuals receive a report highlighting their top 5 strengths. These are the primary areas where a person's natural talents lie and can be leveraged for success.

- *Strength-Based Approach*: Unlike assessments that focus on weaknesses or areas for improvement, CliftonStrengths emphasizes building on what a person does best. It encourages individuals to invest in their natural talents to achieve excellence.

- *Personal and Professional Development*: The insights derived from the test can be applied in various settings, including personal growth, career development, leadership, and team-building. By understanding their unique strengths, individuals can make more informed decisions about their career paths and interpersonal relationships.

- *Customized Strategies*: The results provide customized strategies to help individuals apply their strengths in various aspects of life. Coaches, educators, and managers often use the approach to enhance engagement, productivity, and overall well-being.

Here are brief descriptions of my five specific talent themes from the Gallup Clifton Strengths assessment:

1. Learner:

Description: Individuals with the Learner theme have a strong desire to learn and continuously improve. They find energy in the process of learning, whether it involves acquiring new skills, understanding new subjects, or gaining insights. The journey of learning, rather than the outcome, often motivates them.

2. Analytical:

Description: People with an Analytical theme seek to understand the underlying reasons and causes of things. They approach situations by analyzing data, facts, and logical connections. They value precision and accuracy and are skilled at identifying patterns and making data-driven decisions.

3. Discipline:

Description: The Discipline theme emphasizes structure and routine. Individuals with this theme seek consistency and precision. They create and follow clear plans and routines, and their methodical approach helps them achieve their goals. They excel in environments where order and predictability are valued.

4. Responsibility:

Description: People exceptionally talented in the Responsibility theme take psychological ownership of what they commit to. They are dedicated to stable values such as honesty and loyalty.

5. Restorative:

Description: Individuals with the Restorative theme are problem-solvers who enjoy taking on challenges and finding solutions. They excel at identifying issues and working diligently to correct them. They are driven by the satisfaction of resolving problems and restoring things to their optimal state.

I have a passion for understanding how people are wired, to the extent that I am certified as a DISC and Motivators Analyst. The DISC personality test is a behavioral assessment tool used to understand an individual's personality and behavior, particularly in a work environment.

The DISC personality test categorizes individuals into four primary personality traits: Dominance/Driver (D), Influence (I), Steadiness (S), and Compliance/Conscientiousness (C). These traits are often represented in a circular model, with each trait related to a specific style of behavior. Organizations use this assessment for purposes such as team building, leadership development, sales training, and conflict resolution.

- *Dominance* **(D)**: Individuals with high D scores are assertive, ambitious, and goal-oriented. They prefer control and authority, striving for results and efficiency.

- *Influence* **(I)**: People with high I scores are outgoing, enthusiastic, and persuasive. They enjoy social interaction and are effective in influencing or motivating others.

- *Steadiness* **(S)**: Those with high S scores are calm, patient, and cooperative. They seek stability, consistency, and often excel in supportive roles, emphasizing collaboration and team harmony.

- *Compliance/Conscientiousness* **(C)**: Individuals with high C scores are analytical, precise, and detail-oriented. They focus on quality, follow the rules and procedures, and excel in roles requiring critical thinking and meticulousness.

The DISC assessment identifies the combination of these traits within an individual, providing insights into how a person may react in various situations, communicate with others, or fit within a team or organization. It's a valuable tool for personal development and understanding the dynamics within a group.

I am always learning more about my personality. I show up as a high C and a high S on the DISC chart, which is Compliant/Conscientious. Some of the traits of a high C personality type on the DISC chart are:

- *Attention to Detail*: High C individuals value accuracy and quality, focusing on details.

- *Analytical Thinking*: They rely on logic and facts, making decisions based on careful analysis.

- *Rule-Oriented*: They prefer to follow established rules and procedures.

- *Systematic Approach*: They approach tasks in a structured manner, often creating plans.

- *Reserved and Cautious*: More reserved in interactions, they may take time to build trust.

- *Task-Oriented*: They prioritize tasks over socializing and may prefer to work independently.

- *Potential Challenges*: Inflexibility and an overemphasis on details may be areas to watch.

A high S personality type on the DISC chart is characterized by the following traits:

- *Cooperative and Supportive*: High S individuals are typically team players who value collaboration and support others in their efforts.

- *Stable and Predictable*: They tend to be steady, reliable, and consistent in their behavior, often serving as a stabilizing force within a team.

- *Patient and Understanding*: Their patient and empathetic nature makes them good listeners, and they often take the time to understand others' perspectives.

- *Resistant to Change*: They may be uncomfortable with sudden changes or disruptions to established routines and prefer a more methodical approach.

- *Relationship-Oriented*: Unlike more task-focused personalities, high S individuals prioritize relationships and often work to maintain harmony within a group.

- *Cautious Decision-Making*: They typically approach decisions carefully, considering the impact on others and preferring to avoid unnecessary risks.

I'm very analytical, and I like to have all the information before I take action on something, so I benefited from learning more about how I show up at my best and where I could improve some of my weaknesses, like getting analysis paralysis by overanalyzing things and not taking action. When I discovered more about myself, it was uncomfortable, but I realized that taking action, even when I didn't necessarily feel like I was ready, was key to accomplishing my goals in life.

A lot of REALTORS® do the bare minimum when it comes to education, specifically Continuing Education. But most people in life do the bare minimum. When I was working in manufacturing, that's what I did too, just scraping by, doing the bare minimum. But I decided that was not going to happen in my real estate work or my life anymore! I realized that I could stand out from my competition by going above and beyond, going the extra mile, and doing what other people weren't doing.

To be a REALTOR®, it's 180 hours (in Texas), and then in your first two years, you need 98 more hours of continuing education. I decided that I was going to go ahead and knock those hours out while I was new to the business. I came into the business knowing the statistics that 85% of REALTORS® fail in their first two years.

I also knew that the statistics for most businesses were similar. So, if you can make it through your first two years, then it's more likely that you're going to stay in business. I decided from the beginning that I would set myself up with a solid foundation for long-term success by getting educated and taking advantage of the resources in front of me and available to me. I took the GRI designation, which is the Graduate REALTORS® Institute designation. It is 90 hours of education. If you're thinking of it in terms of a college degree, where you get your Bachelor's degree, then you get your Master's degree; this is essentially the equivalent for real estate. It helps you learn about what you're going to do on a day-to-day basis in real estate. Most of the time, the original 180 hours don't teach you what you're going to be doing daily. It gives you a broad overview.

My instructor was Candy Cooke. She's been in the real estate industry for 40 years as a REALTOR®, and then 35 years as an appraiser, and 15 years as a REALTOR® education instructor.

Another key to success is the opportunity to spend time with and learn from people who know more than you and who are experienced in what you want to be good at. Proximity is power.

Learning from Candy and other REALTORS® from across the state of Texas, being part of Zoom meetings, and being placed into breakout rooms where we could interact and discuss their real-life experiences was instrumental in my growth. I kept taking classes, realizing that if I wanted to stand out, I should take more classes than anyone else I knew. In my first two years as a REALTOR®, I accumulated more education than most REALTORS® who have been in the business for ten years.

I want to become a broker, so I need 900 hours of continuing education and four years of experience in the business. If you have a college degree, some of the hours transfer over toward the 900 hours needed. I have over 470 hours of total education so far in my first two and a half years in the real estate business. I'm on track to get my broker's license in 2025.

Being more professional and competent in the business makes a big difference. There are a lot of people just going out willy-nilly, guns blazing, not really understanding what they're doing. A lot of bad things can happen when you're handling one of the most expensive purchases in any individual's life – their biggest life investment, usually. Make your preparation your separation. So I wanted to take it seriously. I have several certifications, and I am also certified to teach REALTOR® education. Additionally, I am heavily involved in my local community.

One of my favorite quotes is by Henry Ford, "Whether you think you can, or you think you can't – you're right,"

It underscores the profound impact of an individual's mindset and self-belief on their ability to achieve goals or tackle challenges.

Mindset: The quote places great emphasis on the importance of one's mindset. A positive or negative mindset can either propel individuals forward or hold them back.

Self-belief: Ford suggests that the belief in one's capabilities determines the outcome even before one undertakes a task. Those who believe they can achieve something are more likely to put in the effort and persist, making success more probable.

Self-fulfilling Prophecy: The quote touches on the psychological phenomenon where an individual's belief or expectation influences their actions in such a way that it causes those expectations to come true.

Power of Perception: Our perception of our abilities can shape our reality. If we perceive a task as achievable, we approach it with different behaviors and attitudes than if we view it as insurmountable.

Influence on Actions: A person's belief about their capability can directly influence the effort they invest, their persistence in the face of challenges, and their resilience to setbacks.

Understanding and leveraging the power of mindset can be crucial in motivating yourself to achieve your goals.

I got more involved with my local real estate board because I was taking so many classes through them, meeting more of the successful agents in my city and realizing that the most successful tenured agents in the business take a lot of education, and they take it seriously. They're also involved with local politics, local community events, and upcoming growth relevant to the city they live and work in. I focused on getting more tuned into and involved in the community.

There's a committee at my local real estate board called the NextGen Committee that helps the next generation of REALTORS® coming into the business. I started getting involved there and taking classes. I got on that committee to see what it was all about. And the following year, I was asked to be the committee chairperson.

Because of all the education I took and implemented, learning more about social media, growing my online presence, and my overall drive, dedication, and perseverance, I was awarded Rookie of the Year by my local real estate association. It was unexpected, but at the same time, it wasn't. I believe it was all my work the previous three years (An overnight success, ten years in the making!). Those three years of work led to this defining moment. That was one of my takeaways or "Ah-Ha" moments.

Many people don't see all of the effort you put into changing your life. One of the reasons I'm writing this book is because I want people to understand that even though you see a successful person, you don't realize everything that they did to get there. Sometimes, when people look at a successful person, they view it as a far-out, unachievable feat. I want to change that. I want the everyday person to realize that every successful person out there is just as normal as you or me. They have the same 24 hours in the day. They have ups and downs, and they make mistakes; they mess up. It's just as possible and achievable for you or me to achieve the same level of success as Elon Musk or Jeff Bezos.

Anybody who has accomplished that level of success has done the same things that I'm currently doing. They have habits; they have consistency. They read, they learn, they educate themselves. And not just traditional education. Yes, college is good. Getting a degree is good. But if you just go to college and get a degree, and then you go get a job and completely stop learning, you will stagnate. If you don't put any emphasis on personal growth, if you don't put any work into yourself to continually keep growing and changing who you are as a person, then you will NEVER meet your highest potential, and you will never be as successful as you want to be. You are your own worst enemy if you let yourself sabotage the potential you have within you to be the best version of yourself! And as far as I know, you only get one life.

When I first read Napoleon Hill's book *Think and Grow Rich*, I didn't fully understand the concepts. But after rereading it and having also read *The Secret*, I discovered The Law of Attraction, and it all made sense to me!

Think and Grow Rich is one of the best-selling books of all time and is based on Hill's study of successful individuals, particularly those with great fortunes. He molded their practices, beliefs, and behaviors into a philosophy of success. The core idea is that thoughts have the power to manifest into reality, and by harnessing this power, individuals can achieve their goals, including financial success.

- **Desire**: The starting point of all achievement is a burning desire. Hill emphasizes that a strong, clear, and well-defined purpose is essential to success.

- **Faith**: Believing in one's ability to achieve is paramount. Hill stresses that faith can be developed through affirmations and visualization techniques.

- **Autosuggestion**: The practice of repeating positive thoughts and goals to oneself, thereby influencing the subconscious mind to work toward those goals.

- **Specialized Knowledge**: Acquiring and using specialized knowledge in one's field is key. Hill argues that general knowledge alone is not sufficient for success.

- **Imagination**: The ability to create and visualize new ideas and concepts, fostering creativity and innovation.

- **Organized Planning**: Developing a clear and actionable plan, and persisting in its execution, is essential for achieving one's goals.

- **Decision**: Decisiveness and the ability to make decisions promptly and stick to them.

- **Persistence**: The sustained effort required to induce faith and execute one's plans.

- **The Mastermind**: Collaborating with a group of like-minded individuals can create synergy and help in reaching goals.

- **The Subconscious Mind**: Understanding and leveraging the power of the subconscious mind to work toward one's goals.

- **The Brain**: Recognizing the brain's potential as a transmitter and receiver of thoughts and ideas.

- **The Sixth Sense**: An abstract concept that refers to creative imagination, intuition, or the receiving of "hunches" from infinite intelligence.

- **Overcoming Fear**: Hill identifies various fears that hinder success and provides strategies to overcome them.

The book has been renowned for its practical advice and has influenced all types of success and personal development philosophies. It has been widely used by individuals seeking to improve their lives, enhance their careers, and achieve financial success.

Everything that you think is not necessarily true; you can change your reality by changing your thoughts. What you focus on, you attract. As I've mentioned before, I'm analytical and skeptical, so I like to learn about the science behind the concepts. For this, I'll tell you about your reticular activating system, the part of your brain that acknowledges what it sees, and then it sees more of that.

The Reticular Activating System (RAS) is a part of the brain that plays a key role in consciousness and the ability to focus attention. The RAS is a tool that can help individuals focus on their goals and filter out unnecessary information.

- *Understanding RAS*: The RAS is a bundle of nerves at the brainstem that filters out unnecessary information, allowing only the essential information to get through.

- *Goal Alignment*: You can tune your RAS towards specific goals that can lead to greater focus and realization of those objectives. By constantly thinking about and visualizing these goals, you can train your RAS to recognize opportunities that align with them.

- *Influence on Behavior*: The RAS can influence behavior and decision-making. Focusing on positive thoughts and aligning the RAS with desired outcomes can drive behavior that leads to success.

- *Practical Application*: Align your RAS with personal and professional goals. This involves clear goal-setting, visualization, and affirmations that help in conditioning the RAS to focus on the desired outcomes.

If you just bought a brand new car, let's say a VW bug, you're going to start seeing more VW bugs because that is part of your conscious awareness now. It's the programming that we have; how our minds were programmed from an early age is how they're going to stay unless we consciously decide to change them. That's what the law of attraction talks about: you have the ability to attract into your life what you want, and you are already attracting into your life what you don't want without even realizing it. So, being able to consciously curate your days is something that I do through affirmations and declarations. Through my habits, I try to curate my day from the start and focus on what I want to attract more of into my life.

There's another book called *Innercise: The New Science to Unlock Your Brain's Hidden Power*, written by John Assaraf. It focuses on personal development and growth through the understanding and utilization of the brain's capabilities.

- **Innercise Technique:**

  "Innercise" is a coined term that refers to a series of mental exercises designed to reprogram the brain. These exercises are intended to help individuals overcome mental and emotional barriers, improve focus, and achieve personal and professional goals.

- **Neuroplasticity:**

  Neuroplasticity is a central concept in the book. It refers to the brain's ability to reorganize and adapt by forming new neural connections. Unlike the previously held belief that the brain's structure is fixed, neuroplasticity shows that the brain can change and evolve throughout life. This adaptability allows for learning, healing, and growth and forms the basis for the Innercise techniques.

- **Mindset Development:**

  Assaraf emphasizes the importance of *mindset* in achieving success. By understanding how the brain works and using the Innercise techniques, individuals can reshape their thinking patterns, beliefs, and behaviors to align with their goals.

- **Science-Based Approach**:

  The book employs a *scientific approach* to personal development, grounding its techniques in neuroscience and psychology. This provides a tangible and rational basis for the methods used.

- **Practical Application**:

  "Innercise" is not just theoretical; it offers *practical exercises* and tools that readers can apply in their daily lives. These strategies aim to enhance self-awareness, emotional control, and cognitive function, leading to better decision-making and goal achievement.

When I read the book and started understanding the brain's potential to change through the concept of neuroplasticity and how to utilize mental exercises to overcome barriers and achieve personal growth and success, my mind was blown, to say the least! The book bridges the gap between scientific understanding and practical application, making it a must-read for anyone seeking to unlock their brain's hidden power.

In simple terms, neuroplasticity is the ability to change your ways no matter how long you've been doing something, no matter how set in your ways you are, and no matter how old you are; there's always the ability to change. A lot of it is done through little habits. When you understand that and know what needs to be done, you can take small actions every day to change your reality and make your wildest dreams come true.

This also ties into your beliefs about money. One of the biggest things that I've been working on recently is wealth accumulation and forming an abundance mindset.

Tony Robbins is a well-known author, coach, and speaker in the fields of personal development and self-help. I like how he describes an "Abundant Mindset": The abundance mindset is a paradigm that operates on the principle that there is enough wealth, success, and happiness for everyone. It stands in contrast to the scarcity mindset, which perceives limitations and often leads to fear and competitiveness. Tony Robbins has emphasized the importance of cultivating an abundance mindset for personal growth and success.

- *Belief in Plenty*: The fundamental belief that resources and opportunities are plentiful and not confined. It promotes a generous, optimistic, and creative outlook on life.

- *Focus on Possibilities*: This mindset encourages individuals to see opportunities rather than obstacles, allowing them to find creative solutions and innovate.

- *Gratitude and Appreciation*: Robbins emphasizes the significance of being grateful for what one has, which can lead to increased happiness and a greater ability to see opportunities.

- *Growth and Collaboration*: By recognizing that success is not a zero-sum game, individuals with an abundance mindset tend to seek collaboration and foster relationships that lead to mutual growth and success.

- *Positive Impact on Others*: This perspective leads to a willingness to share knowledge, wealth, and resources with others, fostering a community where everyone can thrive.

- *Personal Development and Continuous Learning*: Robbins encourages constant growth and learning as part of maintaining an abundance mindset. By investing in oneself, one can continually adapt and thrive in an ever-changing world.

- *Action-Oriented Approach*: An abundance mindset prompts individuals to take positive actions toward their goals, driven by the belief that success is attainable for everyone.

Tony Robbins' concept of the abundance mindset is a powerful tool that encourages optimism, collaboration, continuous learning, and a focus on possibilities rather than limitations. By adopting this perspective, individuals can foster personal growth and success, not only for themselves but also for those around them. It aligns with Robbins' broader teachings on personal development, where mindset plays a critical role in achieving one's goals and dreams.

The most recent book that really blew my mind was *Secrets of the Millionaire Mind* by T. Harv Eker. It explores the underlying thoughts and behaviors that distinguish the wealthy from those who struggle with money.

1. Money Blueprint:

Eker introduces the concept of a "money blueprint," which is an internal mental map that dictates one's financial destiny. This blueprint is formed by childhood experiences and societal teachings and can be changed through awareness and practice.

2. Wealth Files:

The book contains 17 "Wealth Files," which are principles and insights that differentiate the thinking patterns of rich and poor people.

These principles serve as guidelines to transform one's thinking and relationship with money.

3. Financial Thermostat:

Eker emphasizes that everyone has a financial "thermostat" setting that determines their financial comfort zone. If one earns more or less than this set point, subconscious mechanisms may kick in to return to this comfort level. The idea is to adjust this thermostat to reach higher levels of financial success.

4. Process of Manifestation:

The book outlines a four-step process (*Thoughts* lead to *Feelings*, lead to *Actions*, lead to *Results*) to demonstrate how beliefs about money influence behavior and, ultimately, financial outcomes.

5. Inner Management and Awareness:

Eker encourages readers to develop self-awareness about their money beliefs and to replace limiting beliefs with empowering ones. This includes understanding the difference between an asset-building mindset and a consumption-oriented mindset.

I have incorporated the declarations from the *Secrets of The Millionaire Mind* book into my daily affirmations/declarations, and they are listed below:

"Thank you, thank you, thank you, today is a great day full of love and happiness. I am joyful and grateful for being abundantly and perfectly healthy, wealthy, and energetic. Money flows to me easily and abundantly. I receive all of the amazing gifts that the universe has in

store for me today! I feel fantastic, and I am overflowing with gratitude for my beautiful life!"

THEN I CONTINUE WITH THE FOLLOWING:

"I am a Great Son. I am a Great Brother. I am a Great Uncle. I am a Great Friend. I am a Great Partner. I am a Great Investor. I am a Great Leader. I am a Great Coach. I am a Great REALTOR®. I am a Great Speaker. I am a Great Author. I am a Great Teacher. I am a Great Mentor. I am a Great Communicator. I am Great at Listening. I am Understanding. I am Honest. I am Smart. I am Confident. I am a High Performer. I am Worthy. I am a Success. I am Perfectly Healthy, Physically and Mentally. I keep my Promises to Myself and to others. I choose how I react, and I choose Happiness. I achieve whatever I set as a Goal. I add value to everyone and to everything I do. I live in the present. I am dedicated to being better and improving myself every day."

PLACE YOUR HAND ON YOUR HEART AND SAY THE FOLLOWING DECLARATIONS:

"My inner world creates my outer world."

"What I heard about money isn't necessarily true. I choose to adopt new ways of thinking that support my happiness and success."

"What I modeled around money was their way. I choose my way."

"I release my nonsupportive money experiences from the past and create a new and rich future."

"I observe my thoughts and entertain only those that empower me."

"I create the exact amount of my financial success!"

"My goal is to become a millionaire and more!"

"I commit to being rich."

"I think big! I choose to help thousands and thousands of people!"

"I promote my value to others with passion and enthusiasm."

"I am an excellent receiver. I am open and willing to receive massive amounts of money into my life."

"I choose to get paid based on my results."

"I always think I can have both."

"I focus on building my net worth!"

"I am an excellent money manager."

"My money works hard for me and makes me more and more money."

"I am committed to constantly learning and growing."

TOUCH YOUR HEAD AND SAY...

"I HAVE A MILLIONAIRE MIND!"

I say these out loud every morning when I wake up at 4:30 a.m., along with making my bed, brushing my teeth, breathing, and stretching before I go to the gym. I read ten or more pages from a non-fiction book while cycling on the recumbent bike and then lifting weights for a minimum of

30 minutes, followed by cycling or jogging outdoors while listening to a podcast or audiobook for 45 minutes.

Another important piece to starting my day off right is NOT using my phone for an alarm clock. I have an old-school alarm clock plugged into my wall across the room. I do not get on my phone or look at the screen until after I'm done at the gym. I have my phone on "do not disturb" from 9:00 p.m. until 6:00 a.m. I have my emergency contacts set to be able to ring through, but other than that, no notifications or alerts will wake me up or disturb my sleep.

When I worked in manufacturing, I would use my phone as my alarm clock and have three alarms set. I "snoozed" the first and second one, and then on the third one, I would get on my phone and start scrolling through Facebook and all these other social media platforms. It really started my day off negatively; taking in all of the negative input from the outside world can affect your entire day. Several studies show anxiety being linked to the negative headlines we're constantly bombarded with! It has helped my mental and physical health tremendously by not getting on the phone for the first couple of hours I'm awake during the week.

There are many studies that target the effect technology, specifically mobile phones, has on our well-being, and most center on these factors:

- *Morning Routine Disruption*: Picture this - you wake up, grab your phone, and suddenly, your usual morning routine is out of the window. This can leave you feeling a bit disorganized and stressed out.

- *Rising Stress Levels*: That morning dive into the news, especially the negative bits, can spike your cortisol levels (that's the body's main stress hormone, by the way). When this happens early in the morning, it might keep you stressed for the rest of the day.

- *Cognitive Function Takes a Hit*: Checking your phone right after you wake up could mess with your brain's shift from the sleepy zone to being fully alert. This might mess with your focus, memory, and decision-making for a bit.

- *Mindfulness Takes a Backseat*: Mornings can be a great time for some quiet reflection or meditation. But if your phone grabs your attention first thing, you're missing out on some precious mindfulness moments that are known to ease anxiety and boost mental well-being.

The research takes the excess phone use even further, focusing on something called "Doomscrolling." It's when you keep scrolling through social media or news platforms, soaking up a constant stream of negative or upsetting news. And here's the effects it can have:

- *Emotional Drain*: The endless flow of bad news can leave you feeling sad, angry, or even helpless, possibly fueling symptoms of anxiety and depression.

- *Negative Beliefs Get a Boost*: Seeing distressing content regularly can cement a pretty grim view of the world, making you see everything around you as negative or threatening.

- *Sleep Disruption*: Doomscrolling before hitting the hay? That's a recipe for messed up sleep patterns, thanks to the stress and the blue light from screens.

So, grabbing your phone as soon as you wake up might not be the best for your mental health. It's a good idea to be mindful of your screen time, particularly in the early hours, and maybe tailor your content so you're not constantly bombarded with negative news. Remember, being careful about who you follow and how it affects your mood can make a big difference.

It's still a bit more difficult to do that on the weekends because I wake up a little later, typically between 6:30 and 8:30 a.m. But I believe you must manage your day and be proactive rather than reactive, taking time for yourself in the mornings or whenever you can do it. I prefer mornings — it's like putting your armor on before battle. I believe you must fill your cup before you try and fill anyone else's cup. Taking care of yourself and loving yourself will allow you to serve and love others better. Self-love is not selfish!

I highly recommend the book *Mindful Metamorphosis* by Michele Schalin. She delves deeply into technology and its negative effects on our culture and how to navigate through a world where we can't escape using it. She also focuses on providing readers with the tools necessary to heal from trauma and progress toward a peaceful and empowered future. The concept of metamorphosis, or true change, is emphasized as an essential skill in the modern world.

- *Healing from Trauma*: Addressing past traumas and finding ways to heal and move forward.

- *Metamorphosis*: The process of undergoing significant change or transformation, both internally and externally.

- *Empowerment*: Gaining strength and confidence to control one's life and claim one's rights.

- *Mindfulness*: Being present and fully engaged with the current moment, leading to increased awareness and understanding.

I believe change is the catalyst for growth. Throughout my journey, I've learned that to unlock our highest potential, we must not only accept change but embrace it wholeheartedly. This book reflects on the significance of embracing change and stepping out of our comfort zones, a practice that has been instrumental in propelling me to success.

As humans, we tend to gravitate towards what's familiar, the routines and environments that provide us with a sense of security. But this attachment to the familiar can also be a chain that holds us back from reaching our potential. I vividly recall the discomfort of leaving my dad and everything I'd ever known behind — the only world I had ever known — and stepping into the unknown. It was a jarring shift, but that very discomfort paved the way for transformation.

Embracing change and pushing through the discomfort is where real growth occurs. The transition into the real estate industry was a prime example of this. Learning a new industry, meeting new people, and facing the uncertainty of sales was scary and unfamiliar compared to my previous life. Yet, it was precisely this discomfort that fueled my determination. Every challenge I encountered became an open door, an opportunity to expand my skill set and evolve as an individual.

It's important to remember that growth doesn't happen without discomfort. As I immersed myself in coaching and personal growth and development, I realized that facing discomfort was a requirement for progress. Whether it was adopting new habits, challenging my limiting beliefs, or stepping onto unfamiliar paths, each instance of discomfort became a stepping stone toward my goals.

In the grand tapestry of our lives, embracing change and discomfort is the thread that weaves through every transformational moment. It's a testament to our willingness to evolve, to confront the unknown, and to conquer our fears. As you navigate your journey towards your own highest potential, remember that every step outside your comfort zone is a step closer to realizing the extraordinary life that awaits you. Embrace change, welcome discomfort, and watch your transformation unfold in ways you never thought possible.

At this point in my life, I am living in the present, but also looking towards the future, organizing my days to be the best version of myself. I am a success now, but I believe that there are levels of success, and I'm constantly striving to reach the next level.

I envision myself standing on stages worldwide, sharing my story, insights, and strategies to empower countless individuals to open doors and reach their highest potential. I see it clearly. This is a glimpse into the future I envision — a future of abundance, growth, and giving back.

My desire to help thousands, if not millions, of people comes from a desire to make a positive and impactful contribution to the world. Every challenge I've encountered, and every transformation I've experienced has carved a path leading to this moment — a moment where I can offer a helping hand to those who seek to overcome adversity, unlock their potential, and craft extraordinary lives. Visualizing this future of abundance, I am humbled and grateful for how far I've come. But I recognize that this is just the beginning.

In the years to come, I anticipate writing more books. I see myself honing my craft, refining my message, and expanding my reach to touch thousands of lives around the world. This vision is not a distant fantasy; it's a reality I'm actively creating and curating through dedicated effort, continuous learning, and an unwavering commitment to my own growth.

As I step into this vision of abundance, I'm guided by the knowledge that every challenge, every setback, and every triumph has brought me to this point. With gratitude for the journey thus far and an open heart for the adventures yet to unfold, I'm ready to embrace the future with open arms.

When it comes to the concepts that I've talked about throughout this book, I know that I am still learning about them and that I will never know everything. But the things that I do understand give me hope to be able to accomplish anything that I want to in life. I hope to provide you, the reader, with a guide to start your journey of self-discovery and self-awareness. I hope you can find different tools that resonate with you, tools that can work for you in your life. I want you to be able to accomplish your greatest and wildest dreams and open doors to meet your highest potential.

CONCLUSION/BEGINNING

As we come to a conclusion on this transformative journey, I'm reminded of the incredible path we've journeyed together. From the depths of growing up in a religious cult to the heights of personal success, our exploration has been a testament to the boundless potential within us all.

We confronted the challenges of my early life, discovering how self-limiting beliefs can shape our reality. Through the lens of my upbringing in isolation, we learned the importance of self-discovery and resilience.

My journey of navigating the transition to the real world and the trials of 'normal' life showcased the power of perseverance and the courage to rewrite one's narrative.

I dove into my transformation as health, fitness, and environment became catalysts for the evolution of my mindset. Transitioning into the real estate industry and embarking on a lifelong journey of personal growth highlighted the immense potential that resides within our choices.

We explored the lessons accumulated along the way — habit stacking, education, affirmations, and embracing change — all pivotal in realizing one's highest potential. The significance of discipline, motivation, and high performance underscores the road to lasting success.

I believe you can experience PTSD or PTG, Post-Traumatic Stress Disorder or Post-Traumatic Growth; it's your choice. In the face of adversity, we are presented with a pivotal choice: to be consumed by the weight of our experiences or to use them as stepping stones for growth. It's a decision that determines whether we cultivate Post-Traumatic Stress Disorder (PTSD) or harness the power of Post-Traumatic Growth (PTG). While trauma can leave scars, it can also serve as a catalyst for transformation. Just as a seed must crack open in order to sprout, our challenges can crack open the door to personal evolution. The path we choose depends on our perspective and our willingness to embrace change. In the crucible of hardship, the human spirit has the remarkable capacity to not only heal but to flourish. It's a reminder that even in our darkest moments, we possess the agency to steer our journey toward post-traumatic growth and, in doing so, unfurl a tapestry of strength, resilience, and newfound purpose.

Lastly, as I look to the future, my vision now is to use my experiences to guide others toward discovering their purpose and unlocking their unique potential. I invite you to take this journey beyond these pages. Whether through booking me for a speaking engagement, coaching sessions, or joining me in the thriving real estate community at EXP Realty, together, we can continue to build the lives we've envisioned.

Remember, your potential is limitless, and the open doors to reaching your highest potential are everywhere. Reach out to me, connect with our growing community, and let's embark on a journey of continued growth, transformation, and the creation of the extraordinary life you deserve.

With immense gratitude and anticipation,
Yitzchak Pierson

QUOTES & INSPIRATION

Yitzchak Pierson's 10 Keys to Success

1. Habits
2. Health
3. Exercise
4. Family
5. Education
6. Implementation
7. Preparation
8. Discomfort/Getting out of your Comfort Zone
9. Knowing When to Say Yes
10. Knowing When to Say No

Here are some quotes that inspire me daily:

"Your level of success will seldom exceed your level of personal development because success is something you attract by the person you become." - Jim Rohn

"Transformation requires sacrifice and the death of who you once were; a price must be paid." - Unknown

What is the biggest room in the world? The room for improvement!

When the pain of the current reality becomes greater than the fear of change, then that's when we change, and my desire to change outweighed any of my excuses.

I'd rather live now like most won't so that in the future, I can live how most can't.

Entrepreneurship is living a few years of your life like most people won't so that you can spend the rest of your life like most people can't.

"Turn your mess into your message. Turn your tests into your testimony." - Unknown

"Make your preparation your separation." - Ed Mylett

"I choose to believe in a person's highest potential, not their current circumstances." - Brian Mayoral

"Wherever focus goes, energy flows." - Tony Robbins

"It's hard to be nervous when your heart is on service." - Unknown

"Self love is not selfish!" - Unknown

"Motivation is what gets you started. Habit is what keeps you going!" - Unknown

"If you leave your growth to randomness, you'll always live in the land of mediocrity!" - Brendon Burchard

"Our obsessions become our possessions!" - Ed Mylett

"People don't buy what you do, they buy WHY you do it." - Simon Sinek

"My value was hidden from them because they were not assigned to my destiny." - Unknown

"Whether you think you can or you think you can't – you're right." - Henry Ford

I will persist until I succeed.

I was not delivered into this world in defeat, nor does failure course in my veins.

I am not a sheep waiting to be prodded by my shepherd.

I am a lion, and I refuse to talk, to walk, to sleep with the sheep.

The slaughterhouse of failure is not my destiny.

"I will persist until I succeed." - OG MANDINO

"You are uniquely positioned to best serve the person you once were!" - Damon West

FEAR:
Fantasized
Experiences
Appearing
Real

Success leaves Clues

You were born with potential.
You were born with goodness and trust.
You were born with ideals and dreams.
You were born with greatness.
You were born with wings.
You are not meant for crawling, so don't.

You have wings.

Learn to use them and fly.

    – Rumi

THANK YOU FOR READING MY BOOK!

Here are a few free gifts.

Scan the QR Code Here:

I appreciate your interest in my book, and value your feedback as it helps me improve future versions of this book. I would appreciate it if you could leave your invaluable review on Amazon.com with your feedback. Thank you!

Made in the USA
Monee, IL
23 December 2023

48524625R00077